Praise for
The LifeQuake Miracle

"Finding one's way successfully through great challenge can be VERY difficult. *The LifeQuake Miracle* is a brilliant step-by-step formula for using chaos, whether global or personal, as an evolutionary driver to a greater life. Dr. Toni Galardi gives the reader a dynamic life-giving path for using any crises as a birth to Greater Aliveness, Purpose and Fulfillment."

Mary Morrissey, bestselling author of *Building Your Field of Dreams*

"It turns out that you don't have to hit bottom head first in order to turn your life around. Who knew? Dr. Toni, that's who. Let her be your guide to a happier, healthier, less shaky-quakey life."

Cathryn Michon, author, *The Grrl Genius Guide to Life*

"Dr. Toni Galardi's new book is the bravest self-disclosure I've ever read. In an act of self-effacing honesty, she strips herself naked emotionally then shows you how she miraculously evolved, sharing inspired insights for your enrichment. Not just spoon-feeding her readers, she engages and guides you with originality to embrace changes you may have resisted in the past."

Dr. Robert W. Gough

"Most people I know are resistant to change and this book can help you to understand and evolve. It explains how to increase your productivity and how to increase your ability to remember your dreams to help with change, which is amazing to me."

Michelle Dunn, columnist, author of *365 Foolish Mistakes Smart Managers Commit Every Day: How and Why to Avoid Them*

❦

"The timing of this book is perfect for all of us. It helps us to ask ourselves how we can manifest our highest purpose both in our personal lives and in the workplace, and then it helps us answer our own questions."

Tiffany Seybert, vice president,
Financial Institutions, ABN AMRO Bank NV

❦

"If you want meaning and purpose but fear change in these uncertain times, this is the book to read. Dr. Toni Galardi offers critical elements to guide you through to a place of joy."

Sirah Vettese, PhD, author of *Spiritual Makeover*

The
LIFEQUAKE
Miracle

Awakening to Your True Purpose in
Times of Personal and Global Upheaval

Toni Galardi, PhD

THE LIFEQUAKE MIRACLE: Awakening to Your True Purpose in Times of Personal and Global Upheaval

Published by Wheatmark®
2030 East Speedway Boulevard, Suite 106
Tucson, Arizona 85719 USA
www.wheatmark.com

ISBN: 978-1-62787-826-5 (hardcover)
ISBN: 978-1-62787-802-9 (paperback)
ISBN: 978-1-62787-803-6 (ebook)
LCCN: 2020906797

Contents

Acknowledgements

The journey of delivering this book truly has been like the pregnancy, birth, and education of a child that evolved as I did. There are many to thank. I have listed them not in order of importance but by virtue of how long they hung in there, without blocking my name on their caller ID!

Although this book is an updated, expanded version of the original text, "the same usual suspects" have continued to be part of my soul tribe and support my work in numerous ways. To Diane Miller, truly the godmother of this book, who not only edited countless proposals for this book and its ultimate final manuscript but also held a constant vision for its release when I had lost faith.

To my mother, who gave me life and a love for reading and writing. To my father, who held the light around me through the years of my Cosmic Barbecue.

To Pati Miller, a "sister" who edited my material and assisted me in creating home after home during the perpetual deconstruction and reconstruction of my LifeQuake.

To Merrie Lynn Ross, who as my first spiritual mentor taught me to detach from the outcome of this journey and introduced me to my master teacher.

To Byron Fox, who taught me, in his brief twenty-two years on this planet, the meaning of offering your life in the service of others.

To Michael Raysses and Kimberly Ross who served as unofficial editors, but none the less vital to the endless copy editing this book required.

To Hyla Cass, MD, who supported me both emotionally and medically during the physically challenging phases of my journey.

To John Vosler, a loyal friend who sent me many clients when I had no time for networking my practice.

To my official editor, Geralyn Gendreau, without whom, this book would have been too long and too clinical. I am eternally grateful to you, Gigi.

To all my clients and students throughout the years, who all taught me more about the journey to the Wholy Self, than I ever taught them. To the LifeQuake pioneers who unselfishly gave me their time and their stories to be included in this book: Barbara Marx Hubbard, Ben Johnson, MD, Bill Twist, Boyd Willat, Chellie Campbell, Deborah Merlin, Diane Miller, Hyla Cass, M.D. Luciano Copete, Lynne Twist, Marci Shimoff, Martin Rutte, Suzy Prudden, Tama Kieves, and Tara Moore.

Foreword

by Marci Shimoff

I first met Dr. Toni Galardi ten years ago, shortly after the initial release of the first edition of this book. She had moved to a town near me, and Dr. Hyla Cass, a sister to us both, knew we should meet.

During a long hike, one sunny Saturday afternoon, we shared about our mutual journeys of writing and teaching our messages to help people live their best lives.

I also learned that even before she'd met me, "Dr. Toni" was in the final edits of the first edition of *The LifeQuake Phenomenon* and she chose to include my book, *Happy for No Reason*, as a recommended resource for people moving through their LifeQuakes.

Since that initial meeting, I feel so grateful to Toni for helping me reframe my own LifeQuakes. Leaning on her wisdom and perspective, I see how every shake up I've experienced has contributed to becoming the most authentic version of myself.

One of my biggest tremors came in June of 1998. At the time, three of my books were in the top five on the *New York Times* bestseller list. I had just given a speech to more than 8,000 people and had autographed 5,432 books. The line for an autograph went all the way around the building. On one level, I felt like an author rockstar.

But after I signed the last book, I went up to my hotel room suite, walked over to the picture windows overlooking Lake Michigan, turned around, and fell onto the bed bursting into tears. I'd thought I had everything I needed in order to be happy, but I was miserable. The emptiness in my heart that I'd worked so hard to fill with outer success was as strong as ever. I realized it was no longer possible to fool myself into thinking that just the next success or shiny object was going to bring me the happiness I longed for. While each success may have brought a short spike in my happiness, it would soon fade away, and I'd be on to seeking the next thing. Oh, that hamster wheel that so many of us have been on!

I would call the experience that day a 'LifeQuake'. In the midst of it, I became determined to get to the root of what it would take for me to experience lasting happiness. And my inner upheaval threw me onto a powerful journey that lead to my soul's next calling—studying, practicing, and teaching happiness.

I wish I'd had *The LifeQuake Repurposing Roadmap* in the early days of that journey to give me the deeper context for what I now know was my rebirthing process.

Toni is an expert guide. She's brilliantly taken what she's learned on her own life path and offered it to us as a beautiful example of what a LifeQuake can gift us with. Her personal experience along with her advanced clinical training, her deep understanding of soul contracts, and her background in integrative medicine have led her to become a true healer.

Toni has spoken on stages around the world and has worked one-on-one with thousands of clients going through their own LifeQuakes. She deeply understands how we, individually and collectively, can make a shift to a greater level of evolution on the planet.

This book is unique and powerful, as it will take you step-by-step through your soul's path of progression. You will learn practical strategies to evolve your body, mind and spirit at various stages, even amidst external chaos. And the extraordinary people interviewed are trailblazers and thought leaders, whose stories serve as great inspiration.

If the life you once knew has dissolved, and you've moved into shaky and unfamiliar territory, I strongly encourage you to read this book from cover to cover. It will give you both the understanding and structure you need to have a resilient and passionate life in which you thrive in the new world that's emerging.

Toni is the midwife you deserve when you're birthing the more awakened you. May the process be gentle and lead you to a most exquisite life ahead.

— Marci Shimoff, #1 *NY Times* best selling author
Happy for No Reason, Love for No Reason, and
Chicken Soup for the Woman's Soul

Introduction

Imagine that you are a bit like the Earth for a moment. And like our lovely blue planet, you have many well-defined layers surrounding your core. Instead of shale and rock, some of your layers are made up of obsolete beliefs and outdated programs that have accumulated over the years. The core self is kept buried by these crusty layers. For your core self to emerge, it must push up and through them. These layers of the false self can be dense and hard to penetrate. Resistance occurs as your essence begins to rise to the surface of awareness. Quite an upheaval can ensue when your innate potential finally breaks through. If you recognize that this process is birthing a new you, it is easier to ride the waves of the inner quaking. If you refuse to follow the signs, a major crisis or catastrophe may result.

Shake-ups like these can make you feel as if you're cracking up, when in actuality you are cracking open. In 1989 I coined a term for this experience. I named it a LifeQuake to distinguish this birthing process from how it can look, as just a massive crisis driven transition. It is nature's way of pushing you to evolve beyond outdated identity patterns so that you can live an authentic, fully actualized life. The process can be chaotic and disorienting; it can also arouse tremendous resistance to change. Just as an earthquake shakes not only the ground, but the houses, buildings, roads, and bridges above it, a LifeQuake can rock every aspect of your life. The very foundation and values on which you've built your life, your professional world, relationships, finances, and innermost thoughts and feelings, all can be thrown into disarray. Are you experiencing more than a little upheaval in your own life right now? Think of your friends and loved ones; I'll bet you know quite a few people who've experienced a LifeQuake or are quivering at the shake, rattle, and roll going on in their lives right now.

We've yet to invent elaborate seismic equipment to read the rumblings of the psyche. Most of us pretend not to notice the subtle tremors and wait until a major quake forces us to change. The intent of this book is to help you discover that you actually can recognize when a cycle of life is ending without massive upheaval, even if the world around you is in chaotic transition. Your journey through a LifeQuake need not be slowed down or complicated by resistance.

This is really the thrust of my entire body of work: you can learn to move forward with intuitive knowing and greater ease, possibly preventing even, devastation in your next major life crisis. To do this, you need a specific skill set that allows you to relax your resistance to change, thus becoming resilient and adaptable to whatever life throws you instantaneously. In so doing, you develop an agile, fluid mind.

Contemporary life may be calling you to die to old ways and rise from the ashes, over and over again. In the process, you will learn to be fearless and forward-looking, to approach the unknown with a sense of adventure rather than dread. The ability to adapt to rapid change at the present time is a necessary part of your survival and subsequent evolution.

Do you find however, that when you sense it's time to make a change, that feeling does not always lead to action? Does the lull of the familiar keep you circling around the same old issues, while the lure of hope keeps you scanning for that magic bullet that will solve the problem or quell the boredom? Or, perhaps you go numb with the help of favorite substances and distractions that temporarily ease the pressure building up inside.

Left unaddressed, this inner pressure grows into a rumbling discontent. Boredom, restlessness - an inner tension that has no name - begins to cast a pall over your life. Unchecked, this discontent deepens into a "depression" that handy prescriptions cannot fix. What often remains unaddressed when depressive symptoms arise is this: your soul is crying out for your attention.

Holding on to an obsolete life makes change difficult, but the soul has its own way of breaking your grip. Your innermost being knows what your mind can easily deny or pretend not to see. Every bit of self-delusion must be exposed, even the pockets that hide under a spiritual practice such as meditation. Avoidance of change is futile; put it off and you invite a crisis.

The epidemic increase in the use of antidepressants is masking this eruption from the soul. That is not to say that pharmaceutical treatments for despair and anxiety don't have their place; they most certainly do. However, there is a critical context for holding these emotions that must be attended to, if we are to stay sane in the face of the sweeping changes occurring worldwide. To understand your personal discontent, you might want to take into account the bigger reality of our times: we are both participating in and being swept along by a massive evolutionary moment.

This vastly intelligent force of change is breaking down old ways of being and evolving new forms. On the human front, this is occurring through you and me. It is this irresistible force, this inevitable progression that is calling you inward, to discover your unique purpose, and to take your rightful place in the larger whole.

I know this process first hand. I have been reborn in the desert many times. My physical birth took place in the city of Phoenix, named for the mythical bird that descended into flames so that it could be reborn into a higher form. I came by the model I developed the hard way, fraught with near fatal experiences, when I resisted the call from the future to move on.

The mandate of twenty-first century transformation, however, need not bring on catastrophic crisis. Quantum theory is showing us this, that chaos can be experienced as a natural organic process rather than chronic disaster. This extraordinary, miraculous, birthing process that I have named a LifeQuake can be mastered with the help of the simple techniques contained in these pages.

As you take this journey, an inner structure will build that has the kind of emotional retrofitting that allows you to actually trust chaos, to recognize this deconstruction as fundamental to transformation as Summer is to Autumn. This transformation happens at a foundational level, dissolving old programs so that you readily interpret change as gain, rather than loss. Easier said than done, right?

If you don't have a road map for such a journey, you can get lost in perpetual crisis, a hellish spin cycle of drama and trauma.

What you have in your hand, however, is that very road map—the manual for developing an adaptive mind; it can carry you through this phenomenon called a LifeQuake to a surprising and unexpected destination. I will show you the way by charting the course for you, identifying the obstacles and hazards, pointing out landmarks, helping you read the road signs, and giving you a custom-designed set of master tools. These tools develop a body that is mobile, a mind that is agile, and a spirit that is responsive to the daily demands of accelerated change. They work with your electromagnetic field through accessing light energy. All the parts of self that have been rigid and resistant to change will gently soften.

This is the new paradigm for our evolution: we all are being summoned by the future to become emotionally, mentally, physically, and spiritually fluid. The prolific French writer Anais Nin once said, "We need blueprints for the creation of human beings the way we do for architecture."

This book will artfully guide you through this new quantum-healing frontier. You will be able to develop your own unique, ever-changing blueprint that allows you to build and maintain a vital life. Furthermore, once you've mastered change in your own life, you will become a more effective change agent for others.

If your LifeQuake has not reached a disruptive level, you may be asking yourself if your experience qualifies. Start by taking the questionnaire that follows chapter one. You will see that there are many subtle signs in the early stages. The seven-stage roadmap set forth in this book will serve different functions at different times as you make your way through it. Use it to guide you from stage to stage. Please remember though that this process is not necessarily linear. Quantum healing can happen in an instant. Return to this map when you feel lost and need a safety net or when your journey leaves you feeling as if you've fallen from a high wire.

You will need clearly delineated building elements in each of the seven stages. These will make up your new foundation as an evolutionary being. As you put each building element to use, you evolve from being "defunctional" (one who is holding onto an obsolete identity that resists change) to becoming transfunctional. As a transfunctional being, you learn to foresee and adapt to necessary change, moment to moment. You can achieve change mastery by practicing these tools. Furthermore, I have sprinkled references throughout the text to a multitude of cutting-edge resources to support your body, mind, and spirit during this radical transition.

There are also fifteen interviews with individuals who have pioneered the new frontier of evolutionary consciousness, as well as anonymous stories from clients who trusted me to be their guide as they bravely pioneered their way through the unknown territory of their own LifeQuake journeys.

Before we start, here's a quick preview of what's ahead: in stages one and two, you will discover how to transform the inherent feelings of boredom and depression so that you can gradually release dated aspects of your life and create space for the newness taking shape. The momentum created by these first two stages prepares you for stage three, where you will either consciously make a definitive break from your old life or magnetize crisis to accelerate the unavoidable change that wants and needs to happen.

Do the work in these first three stages, and you will be weaned from any dependence on crisis as a way to bring about meaningful change. Thus, awareness—not catastrophe—becomes your springboard.

Stage four shows you how to integrate the denied parts of yourself into the emerging you; this prepares you to discover your true calling. Stage five teaches you how to create a fluid blueprint that allows you to experiment and become an apprentice in your new life with a clearly defined life purpose and mission. Stage six shows you how to create and live in the spirit of true prosperity that will shift the global paradigm for wealth, so that no one is left behind. Finally, stage seven gives you user-friendly tools that allow you to discover how you knowing your soul purpose will create global change. I highly recommend reading *Chapter 7*, the last chapter, at least a day or so after you finish Chapter 6. It will help to integrate the whole arc of the model.

If this journey sounds daunting, do not be alarmed. We're all standing at the very same crossroads. One path looks solid and well tread, while the other may look unsteady because it's uncharted. I invite you to choose the latter; imagine my hand being extended to you through these pages. Through this book, you have me as your personal 21st century "stage" coach. I am inviting you to open the door to this vehicle for quantum evolving and enter this multi-dimensional adventure. May it carry you safely as you "space travel" through this new terrain.

This unique journey will lead you to your ultimate destiny: a passion-filled purpose, rooted in pure liberation: for both you, and all of humanity.

The LifeQuake Lexicon

In the first version of this book I put the lexicon at the end as instructed by my editor. However, because I created new words for concepts embodied of repurposing your life and restructuring the very cells of your body, I want you to be familiar with these words from the beginning. This makes it easier for you to refer back to this section before chapter one.

Cellar Self: an archetype that comprises all the sub-personalities of the psyche that one has disowned and kept repressed in the psychological cellar. The usual term shadow conveys a tone that these aspects are negative, as opposed to simply being out of conscious awareness. Some of the Cellar Selves contain talents and strengths we have been afraid to express.

Cosmic Barbecue: the transition between the old familiar life and the new one that has yet to be formed. The lack of concrete outer identity that comes with this limbo state forces you to face aspects of self that you fear or judge.

Defunctional Self: acting from an outmoded personality style that is defined by one's outer identity.

Divine Coincidence: synchronistic outer experiences that are triggered by a magnetic pull from the soul to guide you toward your destiny.

Emotional Pulse Check: checking in with your body every few hours to gauge how you are breathing and what you are feeling.

Fertile Soul: defines one's self as wealthy, based on perception, not material assets.

Humane-itarian: one who not only is devoted to the betterment of humankind but recognizes no difference between the helper and the helpee.

LifeQuake: the labor pains of the individual soul birthing into the next level of its evolution.

The LifeQuake Miracle: an unprecedented leap in our current evolution ... one that catalyzes a critical mass of humanity to learn how to adapt and thrive in the face of accelerated change.

Master Blueprint: the structure that replaces outmoded genetic programming and is designed by an adaptive mind that engages and changes as evolution dictates.

Spiritual Depression: the mourning process of an old cycle completing.

Transfunctional Self: the new human whose body, mind, and spirit are agile. As an individualized expression of the Wholy Self, is able to master change by dropping into the subconscious through breathing into the body, clearing any fear-based emotions, and then accessing the quantum field for solutions or answers.

Wholy Self: unified consciousness, our highest potential self.

1

The Heat Wave: Subtle Tremors

Change. What do you feel when you hear that word? For most of us, the thought of change brings on a mixture of excitement, anxiety, or all-out terror. We love the idea of leading a fulfilling life. No one wants to waste his or her potential or stay stuck in old ruts, and yet, most of us struggle with making needed changes. When you look closely at what you're afraid of, you might recognize that what you really fear is the unknown. Inherent to not knowing is the mother of all fears: the assumption that change brings loss. So we bump along, ruled by subliminal fears, and stay asleep to the fact that change is needed. That is, of course, until a crisis hits.

We all tend to gravitate toward what we know rather than venture into foreign territory. Strangely enough, our resistance to change is deeply rooted in our biology. Fortunately, the ability to adapt, to change with circumstances and grow accustomed to new vistas, is also fundamental to our human brain thriving. That's good news, because there is no denying that these are trying times. Like it or not, a radical transition is underway. You may not have a name for it, but it is likely that you're feeling the change I'm talking about, as it plays out in both your own theater and on the world stage. When sweeping sudden changes happen at the accelerated rate that we are seeing today, chaos is always part of the equation.

To the ancient Greeks, "chaos" described the void space where the gods and goddesses were born. In quantum physics, chaos is the state into which an organism deconstructs after having reached its maximum potential, before it reorganizes at a higher level of functioning.

Limbo then becomes that very space where the new you is born from this chaotic transition. If the words chaos and limbo trigger anxiety, keep in mind that you are quite experienced with both states of being. Your first experience of chaos may have occurred when you left home for the first time to enter kindergarten. Similarly, when you started a new job, went off to college, got married, or had a baby, chaos was a feature of each major transition. Even normal events like these involve degrees of chaos. The completion of one cycle compels you to step into the unknown. Each new phase of life temporarily destabilizes you—and yet you've navigated this state of flux many times.

Unfortunately, the evolutionary passage that is occurring worldwide right now isn't as easy to recognize amidst the chaos, however, it has been emerging for quite some time in both subtle to crisis-driven forms. There is no birth certificate to mark this new beginning—and this transition's course is far more uncertain than any pregnancy. We know a pregnancy only happens to women, takes around nine months, and culminates in a tangible result. On the other hand, this type of gestation has no set pattern. It can consume a man's life just as completely as a woman's. It can take a few days, several weeks, or many years and has no sure result, for what is emerging in and through us has not existed before. We are literally creating a new kind of human.

So, what's your challenge in all of this? The key is to learn to consciously evolve without traumatic chaos. And the name of this new kind of conscious evolution, this birthing process, I named *The LifeQuake Phenomenon* originally. I want to define the word phenomenon as it is explained first by Webster: "a remarkable or miraculous person, thing, or event." For the 10th anniversary edition, I renamed the title to make it easier to translate correctly into other languages and because this global transition truly is miraculous!

Although the birthing experience of a LifeQuake is remarkable, without a context and map to guide you, you and everyone around you may question whether this chaos is a good thing. In this new quantum model of change, you will discover how to create miracles with a structured roadmap.

This book will give you the tools to avoid being shattered by chaos, while cultivating your inborn sense of adaptability. It will help you reformat your hard drive of the programs that keep you terrified of change. Chaos itself will become your ally—you will discover that you can trust it and trust yourself to pull through. This is conscious evolution. The pioneering talents and abilities involved are inside of you; they only need be activated and brought online.

To be sure, this is a miraculous phenomenon that has a unique unfolding for each person and his or her circumstances. As I lead you through your LifeQuake, you will learn to let go of what is no longer working, while creating the highest potential in every moment. But you will need a specific skill set to do that. Most of us don't have those skills; crisis-driven change has been our default.

The LifeQuake Repurposing Roadmap unfolds in stages that can be identified. It provides a model as revolutionary as the process it leads you through, lending itself to your unique development however it unfolds. The seven stages will give you landmarks and signposts that point the way, allowing you to understand your new frontier of radical transition.

The mandate is adaptability. Each of us is being called to evolve in this way—to be ready, willing, and able to adapt, adapt, adapt, and adapt again, if necessary. The key "emergent"—or evolutionary development—can be summed up in the phrase "an agile mind." Evolution selects for adaptability; fortunately, adaptability itself can be learned. *The LifeQuake Repurposing Roadmap* will help you do just that.

It is important to note that while *The LifeQuake Repurposing Roadmap* is laid out in progressive stages, it's a model that incorporates and is dependent on a nonlinear dimension in which past, present, and future exist in a dynamic interrelationship. What's important, then, to keep in mind is that your movement through the stages may not necessarily progress sequentially.

Once you're introduced to the model and its seven stages, the next time a cycle starts to end, you will recognize the symptoms more readily. For instance, symptoms such as boredom and depression will no longer be viewed judgmentally but simply as a reflection of what is now "defunctional." The beliefs and lifestyle choices that impede your ability to grow and adapt have become defunct and must die off. This is part of a natural process that allows organic change to occur. In stage one, for example, boredom will become your friend and ally, showing you well in advance that change is necessary. Mastering the skills of stage one will support your rite of passage to the new you; the you who is not just efficient, but masterful at intuiting what changes you need to make, when you need to make them, and then actually making them happen.

Why White-Knuckle It When You Can Rock 'n' Roll?

So how does this "awakening" begin?

The onset of a LifeQuake is usually tough to pinpoint. You might start to notice it one morning when you're startled by your own reflection in the mirror, you look the same, but you don't quite recognize the face staring back at you. As you turn away, you might have a sense that though nothing is technically wrong, nothing is quite right either. So you shake your head and just get on with your day.

Or maybe the first sign surfaces when you hear yourself say something completely out of character, a sarcastic reply to an innocent question, for example. Or, even more upsetting, you find yourself unable to answer the simple question, "How are you?" In moments like these, you glimpse the vague, shadowy outline of a disturbing pattern: you aren't acting like you anymore.

But that's crazy, right? If you're not acting like you, then just who are you acting like? So, you check yourself and, in keeping with the person you think you are, you recommit to being the most vivid version of yourself that you can be. And for a while, you actually pull it off. Or you think you do. But the nagging sense that there is something fundamentally very wrong has now cast a shadow over everything you do. If pressed to describe what you're feeling, you might say that you're bored, overworked, tired, or just plain burned-out. The need for change is obvious, but you hold onto your old life with white-knuckled determination. You wish for security in the way a child holds on to his mother's skirt—innocent, dependent, and totally oblivious. Well, not exactly. You're too old to be totally oblivious, but you're also too entrenched to let go.

In the initial stage of a LifeQuake, boredom is more than a seven - letter word. In this instance, it's boredom with a capital "B." This isn't your garden-variety boredom that comes from hanging around the house on a rainy day, watching too much TV, or the tedium of chores. This Boredom is more complex than that. It is laced with liberal doses of irritability, restlessness, and that weary feeling called ennui.

Stage one begins with a distinct form of boredom with the life you have now outgrown. Signs of change are all around, and they irritate like pebbles in your shoe. If you don't stop and shake them out, you could end up with blisters. Thinking you can ignore them indefinitely might even leave you with a marked limp.

Oh, and the soundtrack for stage one features an old Peggy Lee song "Is That All There Is?"

The Alchemy of Heat

Ego is defined here as the voice in your head that is scripted by old programs. Instilled by your family and the culture in which you grew up, these programs represent early learning on how to deal with "pebbles in your shoes." This voice holds fast to your familiar identity: "It's just a pebble. Get to the office before you take it out." Only you don't take it out once you arrive at the office. In fact, you dig into work and distract yourself from the burning pain in your shoe. You learned to accommodate discomfort a long time ago; diversion is the name of the game. Meanwhile, the irritation around the pebble continues to heat up.

Just as some earthquakes are preceded by heat waves that trigger pressure building in the fault lines, the journey to your soul is fueled by heat. The friction between a dated yet familiar life and the new life that is yet undefined generates a specific kind of inner fire. The intensity of the heat is in direct proportion to your resistance to change.

This is where *The LifeQuake Miracle* is a lot like alchemy, the mythical transformation of lead into gold. For leaded consciousness to turn into golden miracles, the parts of you that are afraid of change must endure the fire of transforming the ego's resistance to change by turning inward.

There is an idiomatic Italian expression, "capa dosta." It means hardheaded or stubborn. If the fear of change was a disease, I could have been the "capa dosta poster child". I couldn't see—much less read—the signs that were plastered with the message "Hello-o, it's time to make a change!" For me, boredom was a subtle fog; it descended imperceptibly and ultimately obscured everything in my life. To make matters worse, I was one of those people who always looked outside myself for substance and sustenance. And why wouldn't I? Raised to believe that if I studied hard, got scholarships, went to college, and became a professional, I would be happy. And I was—at least, for a while. When the glint of that happiness faded, the early tremors of my LifeQuake began. It started with sporadic anxiety.

You might think that as a trained psychotherapist, I would calmly assess the situation and formulate a rational, concrete solution. In fact, my response was typical of anyone afraid of change: I loaded my life with a little more of everything. Where I once had a glass of wine with dinner, I then had two. *What's wrong with two glasses of wine a night?* I asked myself. *Europeans do it all the time*, I reasoned. As a therapist, I knew better; if I had to have it every night, something was wrong. And it wasn't just the grape that I craved.

Prior to this period, I shopped only occasionally. Now I was on a first-name basis at every boutique in town. Then I started working longer hours. I buried myself in overtime, tending to the needs of my patients. To the world, I was the epitome of the responsible adult. I had a demanding job, a mortgage, and a successful husband. I even went to church every Sunday. And when all of that felt flat, I chastised myself for even entertaining the idea that I wasn't happy.

Boredom, Trivialized

We trivialize boredom because we don't understand it as a signal. Although we're tolerant when children and adolescents get bored, in adults it's considered immature or self-indulgent. This narrow-minded understanding doesn't allow us to explore the unique type of boredom inherent to a LifeQuake. In fact, our cultural biases inhibit us from seeing boredom for what it really is—the first phase of an extraordinary metamorphosis. Without this initial recognition, we have little chance of making changes in a timely manner. In *The LifeQuake Repurposing Roadmap*, boredom is a sign that a cycle of your life has run its course.

Through the Lens of a LifeQuake

In each stage of the journey of *The LifeQuake Repurposing Roadmap*, we examine the dual nature of fear-based feelings. For instance, boredom is a transition emotion on the emotional tone scale. At the top of the scale is the feeling of ecstasy. At the bottom of the scale is despair. Boredom is right in the middle.

If you observe how boredom shows up constructively in your body and your life, it can transport you to a higher emotional state, where you can access your intuition and make life-changing choices. Seen in this light, boredom functions like an express elevator in a high-rise building. The momentum you create from making choices that are more authentic can then take you to your emotional "penthouse." Once there, boredom evolves into enthusiasm, a word that comes from the Greek root *entheos*, which means "filled with God." Keeping with our elevator analogy, though, if you allow boredom to trigger addictive impulses and turn to obsessive distractions, like chemical dependency, the internet, or even too much exercise, you may end up in—you guessed it—the basement.

And what awaits you there is an unconscious transition into stage two, where the Blue Light Special is a plate often served cold called Spiritual Depression. Don't worry, though—if you do the work of stage one, you won't have to hit rock bottom.

Let's return to the earthquake metaphor now. If a building has faults in its foundation, it will suffer more damage when stressed by an earthquake. The skills you will discover as we continue will act like earthquake retrofitting; they ensure the building called "your life" can handle the stress of terra firma going through her inevitable shifts. Each of the seven phases requires specific building elements (skills) that help you create a strong foundation—a flexible, adaptive foundation that is free of self-judgment and the paralysis of will that can emerge when you face change. Additionally, each building element helps you build a bridge so you can cross over into the next stage.

Keen Observation

Have you ever noticed how magical things happen when you're on vacation? It's no coincidence that the downshift in your pace that occurs while you're on holiday makes it easier to be fully present. That present-time, in-the-moment awareness opens the door to synchronicity, the magic of divine coincidence. A divine coincidence is an event that your soul magnetizes to guide you toward your destiny. Whether it's a chance meeting with just the right person, or stumbling on to a book that changes your thinking, or just bumping into a stranger who points out a great restaurant where you end up having a fabulous evening, synchronicity matters. But you don't have to get away from your everyday life to experience it firsthand. Divine coincidences show up more frequently when you slow down, wherever you are, allowing yourself to become more keenly aware of your surroundings. By learning to establish a more relaxed pace, you can still get things done and make room for the divine coincidences that will point you in a promising direction.

Another benefit of paying attention to synchronistic events is that they guide you toward preemptive change so that you don't have to bring in crisis to shift gears. Observe divine coincidences throughout your day, both large and small. This practice will provide a gentler alternative to the alarming wake-up call of disruptive events. As you breathe more slowly and relax into every moment, your nervous system becomes more receptive to higher guidance. You gradually release your attachment to life as you've known it, while strengthening your ability to connect the dots of future possibilities.

A pivotal divine coincidence took place for me while in the midst of stage one of my LifeQuake. I was studying with a well-known psychoanalyst on the treatment of the narcissistic personality. He referenced the Greek myth of Narcissus, the teenage boy who saw his reflection in a lake. Unaware that he was seeing himself, Narcissus became enraptured with the reflection in the water. When he reached out to embrace the image, he fell into the lake and drowned.

However, a narcissist is not what pop psychology would have you believe. Narcissists aren't self-centered. In fact, they have just the opposite problem—they are not centered in the self. The myth shows us a self that is defined through a compulsive reliance on an external image. Hearing the instructor describe this personality type, I saw myself and was stunned. Like Narcissus, I was drowning in a sea of public opinion. If I got approval from others, I felt great. If not, my self-esteem was swallowed in an undertow of self-reproach. Although taking this class while awash in feelings of emptiness seemed coincidental, it proved to be a turning point. My pervasive need for validation from others was shaken loose; I began to look within. Unfortunately, though, it took two years and three car accidents until I developed an ongoing meditation practice and began the journey of discovering who I was from the inside out.

Connecting the Dots

Deborah Merlin was well versed in health and healing therapies. She was also a homemaker and mother of twin boys, one of whom had severe attention deficit disorder. She came to me to explore her mission in life. She described the following incident to illustrate where she felt stuck: "I was visiting a friend for lunch when the friend's very large dog put its very large head in my lap and begged for food. If I were not such a people-pleaser, I would have asked my friend to put her dog outside while we were eating. Instead, I kept my mouth shut like I always do. It's no wonder I have a thyroid condition."

In mind/body medicine, thyroid dysfunction indicates blocked communication and/or creativity. Deborah was well aware of this and knew that her desire to be approved of was taxing her health. She didn't know how to listen to her inner voice, however, so I gave her an assignment that taught her how to observe her needs with keen attention. Another exercise helped her apply this same keen attention to what sparked her interest. (See the Toolbox section at the end of this chapter for these exercises.) While using these tools, Deborah observed the excitement she felt while researching an alternative approach to Ritalin for her son. She recognized an unspoken passion for raising consciousness around children with learning disabilities. She eventually wrote a book that details her holistic approach. *Victory over ADHD: How a Mother's Journey to Natural Medicine Reversed Her Children's Severe Emotional, Mental, and Behavioral Problems* has helped thousands of parents better understand and manage their exceptional children. The challenge Deborah faced with her son catalyzed the courage she needed to battle the traditional health-care system. And in finding her mission, Deborah found her voice. Today, she speaks widely on this important issue, offering parents guidance and new hope. In 2014, she published a second book, *A Holistic Approach to ADHD*.

For more information on Deborah's work go to **victoryoveradhd. com**.

Some people have what appears to the outside world like a dream job, and yet they are absolutely miserable. Ben Johnson, a featured expert in the film and book, *The Secret*, was an MD who practiced traditional medicine. Somewhere along the way, he began to feel uninspired by his work. When it ceased to be a challenge, he began to take intense physical risks. Adventure travel made him feel alive again. On one such vacation, while surfing, he suffered a spinal cord injury. This led him to explore alternative medicine, which eventually inspired him to study naturopathy. In time, he opened a cancer clinic in Atlanta. We will return to Dr. Ben in stage seven, when we explore an energetic healing modality that transmutes DNA programming. Dr. Ben passed last year but his work lives on.

Listen to the Quiet Knowing

I discourage people from making radical changes in stage one. To do so runs the risk of silencing the whispers in your present life to which you may need to listen. The unfolding mystery of the new you forming might very well be hiding under these clues. If you are still reading this book, you are consciously ready to embark on this journey. You've realized that seeking external distractions will not ease the early rumblings of your discontent.

Robert was a successful thirty-five-year-old television star who got married when a woman he had been seeing for five weeks became pregnant. Though not in love with her, he took responsibility; this had been deeply ingrained in him by his immigrant parents. Five years and two children later, he came to work with me while in a state of deep dissatisfaction with his life. He had a pretty wife, two kids, and everything money could buy, but like a Chinese meal that doesn't satisfy for long, it left him feeling "un-full-filled."

I suggested that he focus on observing his everyday life, while taking note of what vitalized his body and what left it feeling deadened. He came back a week later with a very short list. When I probed a little deeper, he realized how much he cared about the plight of fatherless inner-city kids. Eventually, this interest led him to open a center devoted to nurturing the creative abilities of these children. He didn't abandon his television career; instead, he found a place in his life for an avocation that fulfilled him on a deeper level.

Not surprisingly, boredom oftentimes brings feelings of irritability and restlessness. Part of mastering this stage is learning how to sit quietly and attend to uncomfortable feelings. Where do you feel the restlessness in your body? Locate that place. Now breathe into it with slow, even breaths. What is this restlessness trying to tell you? What is it that you really need? Engage your feelings with this kind of curiosity, and you will access important information. Any judgmental thoughts that might arise in knee-jerk response to your emotions will be replaced in the process. Learn to observe where feelings live in your body; once you have located that place, listen to their messages. Suspend judgment of such feelings, and you can avoid the tendency to reflexively bail out and find a distraction or another way to avoid the inevitable.

Becoming a Master of Change

Although some of Darwin's theory of survival of the fittest was inaccurate, what remains still relevant (from clinical studies on the effect that fear has on the immune system,) is that the species that can adapt to circumstances as they change tend to survive. Look at the cockroach. It can live in garbage and has existed on the planet for more than 300 million years but it doesn't have the human consciousness that must wrestle with the fear of the unknown and the perception of menacing micro-organisms.

What the tools in the seven stages of your LifeQuake offer are a conscious rite of passage into what I call transfunctional selfhood—a truly liberating experience of you, as a Master of Change into multi-dimensional reality. The prefix "trans" indicates movement, moving your awareness through your conscious, subconscious, and super-conscious mind with such fluidity that it's like operating the gearshift on a Ferrari versus the one on a Mack truck. This allows you to process the information you receive more effectively, lending greater levels of insight that contribute to your highest good.

Stage one leads you through the first step: training your mind to readily cross multiple levels of awareness so that you can recognize, in advance, when you need to make changes. For example, maybe the long awaited promotion or salary increase you just received didn't deliver the expected thrill. Perhaps you actually felt bored at the prospect of moving into this position. As a transfunctional being, you would focus your awareness into that part of your body where the emotion of boredom is present. Then you would investigate the deeper message this emotion is transmitting.

Although your feelings come from your subconscious mind, they are housed in and expressed through your body. Use your breath to surrender into your body for five minutes. Once you feel a shift and your body feels lighter, ask to be shown whether taking the promotion serves your highest good. As you keep breathing into your body, listen closely. Sometimes it helps to ask for a symbol that represents how you will feel if you take the promotion and one that represents looking for a different kind of work. For example, when you focus on the feeling connected to taking the promotion, you may feel heavy and see a symbol of a black cross. When you think about looking for a new career, you feel anxiety but perhaps the symbol that comes to mind is a bridge. What does that tell you?

You may not receive an answer right away. If you don't, ask for a divine coincidence to give you a clue to the right decision and then pay attention as you move through your day. Be patient—remember, this is only the first stage in becoming transfunctional.

In its highest state, transfunctionality fills you with discernment, independent choice making, and a high-adaptability IQ. Once you get to stage seven and experience yourself as operating transfunctionally consistently, you will naturally identify with the Wholy Self—your highest potential of expanded awareness. This awareness dissolves the illusion that you are separate from others. By expanding your awareness to move through your subconscious and super-conscious mind, you are united with the Wholy Self. When you tap into this quantum field by participating in activities, such as sitting in nature, you can truly feel yourself and the entire universe come into an alignment that you've never felt before. Stillness allows you to recognize yourself as the individualized expression of this expanded consciousness, the Wholy Self.

The diagram on the following page shows the transition from the defunctional self to the transfunctional self into the all-inclusive Wholy Self. The characteristics under defunctional self are listed alphabetically but do not transform in any particular order.

Defunctional Self	Transfunctional Self
Tribal Culture Identity	Soul Centered Identity
Duality/Good and Bad	Non-judgment
Shadow Selves Denial	Full Potential Self
Outdated Lifestyle	Constantly Evolving LifeStyle
Bored	Contented
Depressed	Intentional Retreats
Crisis Driven	Adaptable
Fear of Major Change	Foresighted/Visionary
Devoid of Inner Life Tending	Daily Spiritual Practice
Work/Career	Vocation/Mission

Wholy Self

Defunctional Beings
Transfunctional Beings
Unity Consciousness with
All Living Beings

Wake-Up Calls

Incidents occurring in stage one are minor rumblings that signal your life needs to change. Your resistance to this awakening manifests as denial. Ignoring these subtle wake-up calls is a mistake. By ignoring these signs now, the rumblings become full-blown seismic temblors that will later wipe away the ground beneath you. The soul will do what it has to in order to get your attention.

Automobiles are often symbolic of ourselves, illuminating how we move through life. One client, a conscientious accountant, received four parking tickets in quick succession. Not long after, his car got towed when the parking brake gave out, and his car rolled into the street. In his case, the message was to get moving. He was "over-parked" in a life that had become so deeply rutted that he was actually moving backward.

The Wholy Self may draw incidents to you that appear to be coincidental, when in fact they are alarms that it is time to turn within. Life, as you've known it, is over.

One of the most common fears in the early stages of a LifeQuake is "What if I go inside and there's nothing there? What if I'm just an empty shell?" This fear of emptiness is much more common in Western societies. Buddhism and many religions of the East endorse the practice of emptying oneself. Here in the First World, where our minds are racing every waking moment, this concept may be too frightening at this stage. For this reason, if meditation or guided visualization agitates you, simply observe the agitated feeling and notice when it shows up. In fact, observe all your feelings and their relationship to your day-to-day activities. By doing this, you naturally lessen boredom's internal heat wave, while encouraging your intuitive mind to develop.

Remember, if you don't constructively engage symptoms like boredom in stage one with inquiry, you will raise the stakes as you enter stage two, entering it in a mild or deeply depressed state of mind.

Addictions

In an attempt to fill the growing emptiness within, you may find yourself consuming more alcohol, caffeine, or sugar. If you are health conscious, you may even find yourself taking more vitamin supplements or exercising more to increase your waning energy. Though this may actually work for a while, boredom will ultimately reassert itself. Whether you realize it or not, you are subtly withdrawing from an outdated identity. In some people, this may also result in increased substance abuse of one kind or another.

A doctor/colleague referred a client to me, a self-described nutritionist. She initially consulted me to address the issue of her tumultuous relationship with the lead singer of a famous rock group. As the therapy progressed and she began to feel safe, she revealed that her real "day job" was as a $1000-an-hour call girl. For six years, Trina had lived a secret life known only to a few friends. For most of that time, she believed she was performing her true calling. Six months before she started seeing me, however, she noticed she'd gotten into the habit of having a glass of wine before each and every client. As her dissatisfaction deepened, this increased to half a bottle.

Trina professed a desire for calm in her life. In our first session, I had her close her eyes and focus on her breath. When she did, she became agitated and restless. She was incapable of accessing the inner stillness she craved. When I probed her feelings, all she could say was "I feel like there's an earthquake happening in my body."

Although Trina's professional life was uncommon, her experience wasn't. Chemical dependency is only one of many methods we use to distract ourselves from the fear of making necessary changes. Where have addictions popped up for you as a way of avoiding feeling bored? Are you spending more time on the phone, watching TV, or social media? Are you putting too much focus on fixing other people's lives? Addictions at this stage may appear to be very subtle, but the pattern of avoidance can escalate if we continue to shrink away from change.

Lifestyle

As you develop an observant mind, notice if you feel drawn to new colors or different modes of dress. If you are rigidly attached to a certain image of yourself, you'll be tempted to dismiss these impulses as ridiculous.

As the first glimpses of transfunctionality emerge, you'll find yourself doing things that are out of the ordinary. Notice the impulse to break with old routines and habits. Though this may be subtle, it's significant. A case in point: a twenty-six-year-old client still lived at home, four years after graduating college. Her friends didn't judge her for it; several of them still lived at home as well. But the first time she played a Beatles CD while riding with friends in her car, they ridiculed her taste in music.

Intimidated at first, she wondered if her parents had unduly influenced her tastes. I encouraged her to listen to the hip-hop station that was a favorite among her friends, then to listen to the Beatles CD again, taking note of how each made her feel. When she did, she discovered that for her, the poetry in the Beatles' lyrics made her feel more optimistic. The key here is to allow your new interests to be free to develop and reveal what enlivens you.

Health

Two areas that often undergo a marked shift when you enter your LifeQuake are your eating and drinking habits. Remember, your soul isn't the only thing that is morphing—your body is evolving as well. Notice how you feel after eating. You may discover that sweets/sugar, alcohol, or caffeine take a greater toll on you than before. For example, coffee and tea are dehydrating. As your consciousness shifts, your nervous and electrical systems become more sensitive. Even if you haven't noticed, your body will need more water. If so, keeping a bottle of water and carrier with you can be a good reminder. And remember, for now, the changes may be very subtle.

Stage one is also a good time to check in on how you feel after you exercise. If boredom or fatigue sets in where you once felt energized, it's time to adjust your exercise regimen. Altering the length of time or adopting an entirely different program may prove fruitful. I found myself noticing billboards for health clubs after pointedly avoiding them for years. Then, while sitting at a café one afternoon, I met a fitness trainer who explained the beneficial impact that strength training can have on your bone structure. Consequently, I joined a gym and reaped benefits I never would have foreseen.

As my LifeQuake progressed, however, I felt a need to cut back on the amount of cardio exercise I was doing. For a while, my body simply needed to slow down and do something less strenuous. Yoga filled the gap, and my body responded right away. A LifeQuake can both deconstruct and reconstruct your body, sometimes at each new stage, so stay alert to different requirements that emerge along the way. If you learn to listen to your body on a daily basis, rather than follow rote habits; it will sharpen your adaptability.

The Workplace

I've worked with a number of corporate clients who've come to me in the midst of the "golden handcuffs" syndrome, they have high-paying positions, fabulous benefits, jobs they can do with their eyes closed, and yet they feel utterly unfulfilled.

If this sounds familiar, don't be alarmed. The syndrome is rampant at every level of the workforce. It doesn't mean you need to quit your job. Become more present and observant to the specific feelings you are having while at work. Begin to notice which of your responsibilities energizes you. Who are the people you enjoy being around? What time of day are you most alert?

One client noticed that mornings were a killer for him. He was a night person who worked by day as an attorney in a large Chicago law firm, all in an attempt to fulfill his father's dream. I gave him the exercise of jotting down everything he did or noticed that interested him during the course of his day. What surfaced was his interest in comedy: he loved telling jokes at work. The books and movies he most liked were humorous, and he loved comedy clubs. I suggested that he create a stand-up routine, just for the fun of it. He thoroughly enjoyed making people laugh and eventually risked getting up on stage for amateur night at his favorite comedy club. He felt horribly lonely once he got off stage, though, which ultimately led him to join an improvisational comedy troupe. His fellow comedians have since become a second family to him. His avocation eventually became his vocation.

Clearly, not everyone can just up and leave his job. The key to developing transfunctionality in stage one is to use boredom as a catalyst in the keen observation manner we've discussed.

Case in point: Jan was a thirty-nine-year-old computer analyst. Though she was bored with her job, she was adamant about not leaving the company she loved. When she began to observe her day with a keen eye, she noticed an avid interest in the human resources department. Following this interest eventually led her to become an in-house trainer and work part time from home, conducting webinars with the staff. She was able to have her cake and make it rise! By using keen observation, as Jan did, you may just find your passion right where you are.

Relationships

Not surprisingly, as you begin to awaken in stage one, your relationships also will be affected. Boredom may take the form of interest in people who seem more exciting. If you are unconsciously resisting change, the temptation to have an affair with someone new is quite common. Your job is to observe the feelings evoked by these exciting distractions. Do you feel more calm and at ease when you're with someone new? Does that peace carry over into other parts of your life? Or does that sense of fleeting excitement primarily distract you from your growing discomfort with yourself?

On a social level, you may find yourself attracting a different breed of people. They will also shed light on the new life that is unfolding. In stage one of my LifeQuake, I met a psychologist who had shifted her professional focus from traditional psychotherapy into transpersonal psychology. At the time we met, I had lost enthusiasm for the analytic tradition in which I had been trained. I accepted her invitation to attend a conference in Northern California.

While there, I had a deep encounter with a psychologist named Alberto Villoldo, one of the foremost authorities on shamanistic psychology. He then insisted I come to one of his workshops. My mind was blown by this kind of healing. He showed films on a vast array of topics, including psychic surgeries, as well as a man who could channel famous dead painters as he worked the canvas. He also shared his experiences in Peru, where he had studied shamanism. I didn't know it at the time, but meeting Alberto was a divine coincidence that became pivotal to my destiny. Though we never met again, two years later another series of divine coincidences led me to Peru, where I began my own shamanic training.

People or organizations that you encounter now may catalyze transformations yet to come. Pay attention to everything that interests you, even when it seems that very little interests you. Today's seemingly insignificant introduction can be tomorrow's vehicle for change.

Building Elements

Once again, you're building a new foundation that enhances adaptability and mobility so you can move through rapid change with the least amount of resistance. To return to the retrofitting metaphor we used earlier, in stage one you're constructing a new home that will be able to get through an internal earthquake. You want to use building materials that will endure, should a massive amount of pressure come up from underneath and rock the foundation. The "home" you are consciously building when you go through a LifeQuake will be able to support the massive changes that this evolutionary process is creating in your life. The building elements presented here will provide the psycho-spiritual retrofitting you need. In stage one, those building elements are: *keen observation* and *listening*.

Truth be told, as we have experienced the effects of disastrous climate change and the restructuring of the entire world, this inner retrofitting will help us all adapt to national and global LifeQuakes as well.

Here is a suggestion for expressing your intention for stage one: Command your higher wisdom, "Bring me experiences that will best help me master the building elements of *keen observation* and *listening*." By practicing this intention, you won't feel victimized by wake-up calls—because you have consciously asked for them. In fact, this level of intention turns them into divine coincidences. Although sudden events may initially feel disruptive, if you're listening to your life as it unfolds, you're a lot less likely to resist and create more friction. This allows the wake-up calls to move you onto a path that is aligned with your destiny. You can quickly see how these events are actually meant to catalyze the building of your new foundation.

For example, let's say you're at work. You're distracted and make an inflammatory remark. Your boss calls to reprimand you. Instead of blaming the person who reported you, you observe the event as a sign, and then notice how much more irritable you've been lately. You ask yourself "What's the message here?" and then you listen for the answer.

The Toolbox

Here is an exercise to help you cultivate the ability to listen, while keenly observing your inner and outer life.

Note: Although there are exercises and tools sprinkled throughout every chapter, I have added some tools in the form of a 10-hour audio teleclass that coordinate to each stage of this model and can be found at no cost on my website, drtonigalardi.com when you join *The Life-Quake Soul Purpose Tribe* at this link: **drtonigalardi.com/lifequake-miracles-tribe**.

Mastering the tools of stages one and two make the later stages easier to negotiate. If you've not learned to surrender to the more subtle fear-based emotions in stage one, resistance will manifest itself as feelings of shame, rage, and panic in later stages. Thus, practicing the tools of this stage allow you to move on more freely.

Exercise I: Lights, Camera, Action!

Before you get out of bed to start your day, while your conscious mind is still barely merged with your subconscious, close your eyes and think about three things you are truly grateful for. Feel the emotion that this evokes for at least 17 seconds. Now, scan the day ahead. For example, imagine yourself having breakfast. Now surround that image with golden light. See, hear, and feel yourself centered in this calm place. Continue projecting this healing energy while you imagine yourself driving to work, taking meetings, etc., while in a centered, nonresistant state of peace. With your eyes still closed, experience yourself encountering challenges, such as dealing with your boss, while paying close attention to your feelings. As feelings arise, breathe into them, listening for messages from within your body as to how to respond.

As you interpret your body's messages, act on them in your life with authority. Commit to responding to what your body has conveyed to you. Doing this exercise every morning is a form of self-hypnosis; you are programming your mind while in the theta realm, in the pre-waking up state. This practice will sharpen your ability to fluidly adapt to any demand that arises during the day. I have been using this exercise with my clients and seminar attendees for the past twenty years.

Those who use it consistently report how effectively this practice facilitates their day. By taking these few minutes to center and project yourself into the events of your day, you essentially give yourself a spiritual heads-up.

Bookend this exercise by taking fifteen minutes at the end of the day to review your experiences. Remember what you felt as you were doing each activity. Pay attention to even the most mundane, seemingly insignificant activity, such as brushing your teeth. Were you rushed, already feeling pressured to get out the door on time? Now release your observations with forgiveness toward yourself in those instances where you went into an old stress response. This allows you to come into the next day brand new. Done with regularity, this exercise also teaches you to be more observant of what you are feeling in the moment, while releasing your feelings as they arise. When you scan the day after it is over, you can also observe the divine coincidences you may not have noticed while they were happening. You can also be guided in this exercise by listening to it on the *The LifeQuake Repurposing Method* audio recording that can be purchased on **LifeQuake.com**.

Developmental Steps to Change Mastery in Stage One

In all mythic stories, the gods give the hero tasks to perform that will help him develop certain skills. In time, these skills allow the hero to experience the realization of the gods within. *The LifeQuake Repurposing Roadmap* is a process of restructuring you into the next level of your evolution consciously, and it is also a hero's journey. Each step on the path informs the next step. It is in the initial failure and eventual mastery of certain steps that the hero ultimately evolves. Without failure, there is no vulnerability. Without vulnerability, there is no courage. Without courage, there is no morphing into the authentic ever evolving you. Given that the stages naturally overlap, I have listed the steps that prepare you for the next stage of your LifeQuake.

- ✓ Allow your daily pace to ease into slower motion, decreasing artificial stimulants that over rev your motor.

- ✓ Observe what energizes you and what deadens you.

✓ Observe where it is that you hold fear-based emotions in your body, and direct radiant light into those places daily.

At first blush, you may feel inadequate in your mastery of these steps; that's to be expected. Keep in mind the steps are the way you utilize the building elements of each stage. For example, in stage one we observed boredom as a means of accessing its opposite, interest. By discovering what interests you now, you can refocus your attention on what evolves within you as you move into stage two.

How to Clarify What Stage You Are In

If you feel confused as to what stage of your LifeQuake you might be in, you may want to go to LifeQuake.com and you will receive *The LifeQuake Questionnaire and Asssessment.*

Note: The LifeQuake Questionnaire is not a scientific assessment of your psychological health. It was constructed based on those clients and workshop participants who shared with me what they encountered as they went through their LifeQuakes. Yours may involve something other than what is described here. Merely use this questionnaire as a comforting guide for reframing the extraordinary experiences you may have mislabeled as "dysfunctional" on this journey. Keep in mind that this is not a linear model, therefore, you may relate to several of the stages.

2

The Deep Freeze:
The Winter of Your
Discontent

All changes, even the most longed for, have their melancholy, for what we must leave behind us is a part of ourselves. We must die to one life before we can enter another.

~ Anatole France

Onset

Your crossover into stage two occurs when the strategies you used to quell the boredom no longer work, leaving you with the feeling that you are simply going through the motions. Your passion for life is nowhere to be found. Nothing really interests you anymore. Though your life may look the same from the outside, on the inside you feel a profound numbness, as though someone carefully took an ice cube from its tray and rubbed it all over your heart. Believe it or not, this is good news.

What It Appears to Be

What does it mean when you suddenly stop feeling alive to the present, thankful for the past, or optimistic for the future? You might be in a LifeQuake; you might not be clinically depressed after all, no matter what your doctor tells you. You may feel depressed. You may even look depressed. But you are not depressed in the traditional, clinical sense of the diagnosis.

For Diane Miller, international education consultant, stage two began during the holidays. Christmas was always her favorite time of year.

The snow-flocked tree, artfully surrounded with candy-striped boxes, could buoy her spirits, no matter what else was going on in her life. Not so, once her LifeQuake began. She went through all her yuletide rituals, but the holiday cheer seemed to have disappeared. She woke up on Christmas morning and felt absolutely nothing: nothing for her husband, nothing for her family. "Just a flat EKG" is how she characterized it. "I knew I was in trouble when my sister knocked over a glass of cabernet and a set of lit red candles onto my new white carpet, and yet I felt nothing. Even my compulsively tidy perfectionist had gone numb. Nothing could touch my apathy."

For some people who are not at all prone to depression, the restlessness of stage one can turn to anger now. If you continue to resist acknowledging that it's time to make a change in stage two, the buildup of anger can lead to catastrophic change in stage three. The unrecognized wake-up calls of stage one are amplified in stage two. For example, a slew of parking tickets becomes a chain of fender benders and near-miss accidents. If you continue to stay unconscious, a major car accident or two may be ahead for you. In my case, it took three to get my attention. When it's time to make a change, everyone responds in his or her own unique way. Learning how to prepare for the end of a cycle in your life is paramount. The journey is far less devastating when you are mentally and emotionally prepared—what I like to call being "change friendly." I've seen people approach major life change so readily and well-equipped that they experience a feeling of exuberance and relief upon letting go of what is no longer life-giving. However, for most, unless you are working with a coach or therapist who can recognize the distinctions between death of an old way of life and clinical depression, the journey through this stage can be scary.

What Really Is Happening

In order to develop an agile mind that changes readily, rather than being forced to change by a crisis, old beliefs and programs must be challenged. Most people who fear change are very identified with the central belief—and a core feeling—that change equals loss. As you develop the observer who simply witnesses your thoughts, you begin to realize that you are not your thoughts. As you wake up to this understanding, you begin to reconfigure your sense of self to come from inside - out rather than outside-in. For example, up until now, you may have seen yourself through the eyes of the world outside—a mother or father, a lawyer or accountant, someone's spouse or child—external identifications are easy to find.

As you relinquish your attachment to your former identity, quite naturally, you experience loss; a death process takes place. Like a snake, you're shedding an old skin. As your values change, your old picture of success is redefined, making it look gray and alien. In the existential game show of life, the question you might ask is: "If not this, then what?" Nature gives us so many teachings on this death-rebirth process. Who would imagine that a creature, with that heavy body and cumbersome legs like the caterpillar, could become a radiant, flying monarch? The winning answer is that inside the "caterpillar-you" that feels weighed down by your defunctional self, is a new you yet to be born.

Tremendous fear can show up in this transition. You've got one foot planted in your old life while the other is dangling in midair. Two things are at odds here: your soul is pulling you inward so that transformation can take place; and the ego is doing its best to hold onto what you know. Your subconscious will do all it can to resist. Attachment to outer things may even increase as reverberations of "It's all you have, baby!" move through your body and mind. All of this is driven by the need to maintain the status quo. Meanwhile, your soul's inward pull may cause fatigue or malaise. With all of that happening at once, is it any wonder you'll be driven to seek something—anything—to stabilize yourself?

Addictions

Numbing out to life can't be a good thing, I thought, remembering the way I used food to anesthetize myself as a teen. When the pain and isolation I felt at being different from my peers grew unbearable, I reached for the one constant friend I had—food. Only this time I wasn't eating to numb myself from emotional pain; I was already completely numb. None of the things that usually gave me a quick fix of euphoria worked anymore—not the chocolate, not the cookies, not the pasta. In fact, for the first time in my life I had to force myself to eat. I was starting to lose weight—a lot of weight—and that scared me. I made myself eat more carbohydrates, just so that I wouldn't get too skinny. *Imagine that,* I thought, *me, having to force myself to eat!*

Instinctively, I knew that a fundamental shift was happening. Only months before I had been drinking two glasses of wine every night; now, I couldn't bring myself to drink a single drop. Night after night, the fine Napa wines my husband and I had bought on our trips to Northern California sat in the wine rack, gathering dust. New cravings emerged: Mexican food, large quantities of milk, yogurt and cheese. And still my weight dropped.

The food cravings were an attempt to stay grounded as my body began to regress. My appearance literally began to resemble that of a prepubescent girl. I began to look at myself with a clinical researcher's eye (when I wasn't afraid I was losing control of my metabolism, that is) and sought advice from my physician. He ran tests on my thyroid that checked out fine and prescribed Xanax for my anxiety.

As my ability to observe myself on a behavioral level sharpened, I began to focus on the nature of my thoughts. The more I watched my thoughts, the more I wondered who was doing the watching. For years I'd kept a replica of Rodin's *The Thinker* on my coffee table. I had totally bought the Cartesian view: "I think, therefore I am." But now I felt compelled to ask: Am I the observer or the thinker? It was starting to dawn on me that I had no tangible sense of who the "I am" was anymore.

Nothing brought me joy any longer, and although I appeared to be merely depressed, I sensed that on a deeper level, something inside me was dying. I had indeed entered the winter of a very confusing discontent. At the age of twenty-eight, I began to feel my life was over. It all seemed so crazy. Nothing on the outside looked any different—I still had a full-time practice, kept two offices, was married, and socialized in the community. But now, on the inside, I felt separate from it all. That feeling deepened to the point that I even felt separate from the thoughts moving through my mind.

Then I became very aware of a part of me I called "the watcher." Though the watcher could hear the voice of self-condemnation running its relentless commentary in my head, it did not judge. The watcher simply observed. Could my inexplicable weight loss be a physical manifestation of this separation process going on in my mind? I theorized that perhaps I needed to go back to a childlike state in order to birth a new me.

Although others were very worried about me, I began to trust that I had stumbled onto something that wasn't documented in the traditional psychological literature. I was convinced this condition was distinct from clinical depression or an eating disorder. My body was morphing into a new state, but first it needed to go backward and re-parent itself, while a new foundation was building in my psyche. Perhaps this explained my sudden attraction to milkshakes, the slurping was so incredibly comforting. Something about the action of sucking and the sweetness of the milk as it moved down my throat ... I surmised that I had unconsciously created an adult adaptation of breast-feeding. Alcohol simply wasn't age-appropriate to the reconstruction that was taking place in my consciousness. But who would believe this? What if I was deluding myself—or worse, had lost my mind?

My weight eventually stabilized at 108; I had lost twenty-two pounds. I wrote a paper about my ordeal titled *"From the Shadows into the Light: A New Category of Eating Disorder"* and presented it at a conference for the California Association of Marriage and Family Therapy. Thirty therapists signed up for my workshop. A number of the therapists in that group shared similar stories from their caseloads. The pieces of a puzzle I didn't even know existed began to come together in my mind. I realized how deeply the family programs that shape a person's identity affect him or her during a spiritual transition. For example, if lack of healthy nurturing from your mother did not dovetail into healthy nurturing of self in adolescence, addiction is all the more likely to show up in your teenage years. Likewise, those who did not challenge family beliefs in their teenage years faced a more profound crisis when their authentic identity began to emerge in a LifeQuake.

When my LifeQuake began, my body expressed the spiritual transition physically by getting lighter. When I went through stage two again at a later time in my life, I gained weight. Any number of addictions can be triggered during such a transition. It is not uncommon for addictive habits we might have developed in stage one to escalate as we go through stage two. If you are already in recovery from some kind of previous addiction and relapse occurs, it may not be the typical relapse if a LifeQuake is emerging.

The gift of addiction in *The LifeQuake Repurposing Roadmap* is that it can actually accelerate the process of stepping into the core self. The clarification that is being called for involves relinquishing everything that is not authentic anymore. This means letting go of dependence on our family and the identity we internalized while growing up. Ethnic beliefs, religious training, and whatever "software" we have downloaded from the world, including bonding patterns, are examined and evaluated from a fresh, individual perspective. For example, a man may have internalized his father's pattern of drinking to avoid pain, only he uses pot instead of alcohol to numb out. A LifeQuake might very well wake him up out of the delusion that pot, in this instance, is any less harmful than alcohol.

In stage two, the soul emerges as a witness to all of the ways you identify who you are. Without this separate witness self, the ego can have you convinced that your worldly identity is the real you. Through the narrow lens of the ego, ending a relationship, quitting or getting fired from a job, or entirely jumping ship on a career path can feel like you are literally dying. The reflex to avoid death is a survival mechanism that is hardwired into us. The ego mind doesn't know how to make a distinction between the threat of physical death and impending psychological death. For some people, the ego becomes consumed with the desire to die at these transitions; thus, suicidal thoughts are not uncommon. In order to negotiate this stage consciously, it is crucial to develop the witness—the watcher of your mind—the part that can recognize that a cycle is coming to a close, and that all endings are beginnings.

The journey of becoming the witness self is an evolutionary process. Few people in stage two are able to willingly feel through this death process without resistance or the need for addictive substances. Further, the compulsion to stimulate dopamine or excitement does not always come from substances. It may temporarily feel better to distract yourself through social media or dating sites than to feel this deadness.

Most of us do everything we can to deny or avoid psychological death. Like the cycles of nature, when autumn comes, seeds are planted and winter brings the dormancy necessary for new life to come in spring. Attempting to force our own agenda by artificially stimulating growth in a death cycle is like trying to stop leaves on a tree from dying. Imagine planting in the middle of winter. Would you expect a crop to pop up under a blanket of snow? What nature teaches us through its seasons is that entropy is a natural state in all of life. When our consciousness has reached an end point in a cycle, we must let go of our own dead leaves in order to evolve into the next level of consciousness.

Unfortunately, we often resist because letting go of the dead leaves means letting go of things we are quite attached to for our sense of identity. This might include your SUV, corporate benefits, and even spouses. However, the dead leaves that are even more difficult to let go of are internal—our treasured beliefs about whom we think we are.

Winter in the Workplace

The onset of stage two can have many different manifestations. For Maria, the deep freeze showed up in her career. An entertainment lawyer, her nickname around the office was Mighty Mouse. Difficult clients were her specialty; she could be counted on to save the day, even in the most perilous circumstance. Her caped-crusader identity kept the fault lines in Maria's foundation from showing. Work was an oasis from the daily challenge of a long-term relationship that was no longer nurturing. The minute she walked into the office, her intimacy-challenged boyfriend ceased to exist. In time, she began to sacrifice good health habits. Her close friends were concerned that she'd become a workaholic.

All that changed once her LifeQuake began. At first, she simply found herself bored with her celebrity clients. Their challenges no longer interested her and rescuing them no longer brought the old thrill. As boredom devolved into outright annoyance, she became uncharacteristically blunt when dealing with their demands. It became easy for her to say no, rather than to roll out the red carpet for clients who'd become accustomed to the star treatment. A casual observer might have viewed her cool, detached approach as highly professional, but Maria was troubled by it. One morning she climbed into her car and looked in the rearview mirror—a vacant stare peered back at her. "It was as if I'd become one of those zombies in *Invasion of the Body Snatchers*," she said.

Many of the people I interviewed had similar experiences in stage two. Our feelings are essential to our humanness; when they go numb or vanish we feel inhuman, even alien. But as we let go of the old satisfactions and the outer world as the source of our fulfillment and identity, we see that this stage of emotional detachment is a necessary transition. Unfortunately, very few people understand the difference between the type of emotional void that accompanies a spiritual crisis and the diminished effect that attends clinical depression, so they turn to medication when this winter cycle begins.

Marc consulted me during stage two of his LifeQuake, while he was still working as a marketing director of an ad agency. His presenting complaint was that he had started smoking pot on a daily basis. Ostensibly, he was "coping with the blues" that he felt about his job. Although he had initially come to me for career coaching, it was clear that he didn't just want a less stressful job; he wanted to find meaning in his life. In the past, marijuana had opened his creative channels, but it no longer worked as his muse. I gave both Maria and Marc the same assignment: follow the sensation of numbness, and make it into an actual character you can engage in a dialogue.

We all have many sub-personalities. Giving them a voice brings awareness and permission to all parts of us. Who is the who, who is dying? Who is it, who is bored? Who is it that is numb, annoyed, or downright mad? Give each a name. Talk to each one. Acknowledge how that sub-personality has served you. It may help to dialogue on paper as though you were writing a script. When you ask a question, you can name it *Watcher*. Whoever the sub-personality is that is present, write its name and the answer next to it. Then, in your journal (that you may have begun in stage one), write a eulogy for each one, just as you would an old friend. For example, write a good-bye speech to the pleaser or the ever-present critical judge, and speak it out loud. Send a letter to your escapist self, the one who never wants to confront uncomfortable feelings and who is driven toward pleasure at all costs. Keep in mind that none of these parts actually disappear. By acknowledging them though they can change into a more effective authentic aspect of you that allows your fullest potential to be expressed. After commemorating the character you are consciously allowing to die, call in a symbol to represent a more adaptive sub-personality. For example, you might replace the critical judge, whose vicious thoughts act as a sword and cut deeply into your self-esteem, with a sword that represents discernment—the ability to sever old habits that hide the essential self. When the symbol appears, draw or describe it in your journal.

These letters may take some time. Let whatever is dying and emerging reveal itself to you organically in various situations.

Lifestyle

Gianna was an accountant with one of the Big Eight accounting firms in Manhattan. She always turned to fashion when she needed an escape from her routine job. As she entered stage two of her LifeQuake, she found herself rushing to her favorite Fifth Avenue shop for a quick fix at lunch. This attempt to thaw her winter of discontent didn't give her the same expected rush. Even her favorite designer's spring collection left her unmoved. I suggested she do the eulogy exercise and ask the part that no longer enjoyed clothes shopping binges, what is it longing for? As she consciously surrendered her familiar and comforting addiction to clothes, a new voice emerged, a voice that guided her to visit thrift shops. Here she found a new wardrobe for the budding self that surfaced as her inner landscape defrosted. She no longer felt compelled to blow an entire paycheck on the latest couture to jolt her enthusiasm or gain her coworkers' admiration. As she got more in touch with this voice, she discovered that she actually preferred vintage clothing she could buy from an online consignment store or even Goodwill. And unlike her former fashion-queen voice, this new voice spoke when she really needed new clothes, rather than whenever she was feeling empty. As you do this exercise of talking to the compulsive habit part that is dying, ask this part what is wanting to emerge from this craving now?

Solitude or Prozac

So you're in stage two, your old addictions aren't sustaining you anymore, and you're no longer feeling emotionally alive. How can you be sure you're not clinically depressed? Here are a few questions to ask:

+ Am I longing for a more meaningful life?

+ Are my values changing?

+ Am I no longer comfortable with certain old friends or long-time intimates?

31

⁕   Am I finding myself needing more solitude?

A yes answer to any of these questions is a sign that the feeling of being depressed is an indication that life as you've known it is coming to an end.

So how do we embrace this relationship with death in a culture that is hell-bent on cheating death? How do we endure the winter of discontent when the outer world demands a sunny personality? How do you know for sure that it's not time for Prozac?

The answer, although direct, can be difficult to face. You begin to consciously examine what is really defunct now and needs to be let go so that you can experience a rebirth in the later stages of your LifeQuake. Without this deliberate inquiry, what is defunctional becomes dysfunctional. For instance, let's say your job or livelihood needs to be restructured. If you don't attend to the need for change, you may find yourself avoiding it by turning to social media or watching YouTube for hours at a time as a way of numbing yourself.

One of the classic definitions of clinical depression is the suppression and repression of active emotions such as anger and guilt. This repression induces a passive, helpless state. Additionally, clinical depression often incapacitates individual choice, making it nearly impossible to be proactive without some kind of biochemical intervention to rebalance the brain. By way of contrast, if you process the parts of you that are dying with conscious intent now, you will activate an expanded awareness as you withdraw from your familiar life. If you medicate yourself with drugs, however, you may douse the alchemical fire that is burning away your defunctional self. Everyone has a different tolerance level for this deep and complex journey, and in some cases, a little help from antidepressants may actually facilitate the adjustment, especially if the letting-go process becomes overwhelming. If this is the case for you, I suggest seeking the help of a psychiatrist who will look with you at the issues you are confronting before writing a prescription. Telemedicine has made seeing a trained clinical professional easier. Your family doctor isn't trained for this; consult a psychiatrist who is also a psychotherapist.

Health Issues

Medications are not the only solution that can actually slow down the acceleration that is taking place when you are in the second stage of a LifeQuake. To counteract the characteristic lethargy, you may be tempted to boost your waning energy with even more coffee, sugar, or nicotine. If you were health conscious to begin with, you will feel even more urgency to exact extreme measures to get those endorphins moving again with megavitamins, exercise, and seemingly healthy drinks loaded with stimulants.

Resisting the mandate to slow down and withdraw your energy (part of the natural process at this stage) may take a toll on your immune system. People who don't listen to their body's need for gearing down may run the risk of developing any number of autoimmune disorders in stage two. Auto-immune disorders are very symbolic because they are conditions where the body is attacking itself. Examples include Chronic Fatigue Syndrome (also referred to as myalgic encephalomyelitis or The Epstein Barr virus), fibromyalgia, and Hashimoto's thyroiditis. If appropriate steps to change your life aren't taken, these conditions take an even higher toll in stages three and four.

Chronic Fatigue Syndrome (CFS) may manifest as one of many possible illnesses. For example, adrenal exhaustion, in its infancy, may look like Chronic Fatigue Syndrome. A thyroid or hormonal imbalance can be mistaken for CFS. For an accurate diagnosis of CFS, an individual must demonstrate debilitating fatigue and test negative for these two endocrine imbalances. There are additional diagnostic criteria, four or more of which must be present concurrently—substantial impairment in short-term memory or concentration; sore throat; tender lymph nodes; muscle pain; multi-joint pain without swelling or redness; headaches of a new type, pattern, or severity; unsatisfying sleep; and post-exertional malaise lasting more than twenty-four hours. These symptoms must have persisted or recurred during six or more consecutive months of illness and must not have predated the fatigue.

Fibromyalgia Syndrome (FMS), as defined by the Fibromyalgia Network, "is a widespread musculoskeletal pain and fatigue disorder, the cause of which is still unknown. Fibromyalgia means pain in the muscles, ligaments, and tendons—the soft fibrous tissues in the body. Most patients with FMS say that they ache all over. Their muscles may feel like they have been pulled or overworked. Sometimes the muscles twitch and at other times they burn. More women than men are afflicted with FMS, and it shows up in people of all ages."

Besides Hashimoto's thyroiditis disease, there are other thyroid diseases that can show up in a LifeQuake such as hyper or hypothyroidism. Blood tests will determine a differential diagnosis. Again, if the onset occurs after your LifeQuake has begun, it has a symbolic message. The neck in body-mind medicine represents the physical transition between the head (our intellect) and the body (our instincts). Resistance to listening to our gut instincts can create physical blockages that eventually lead to neck imbalances—in my case, three whiplash accidents and antibodies that attacked my thyroid.

Just as the symptoms of real clinical depression can appear the same as spiritual depression, the emergence of an autoimmune disease can have a psycho-spiritual root, especially if you are in a LifeQuake. I don't think it is accidental that many of these autoimmune diseases (and chronic viruses like HIV and HPV) began to show up in the Western world in the '80s, along with acute viruses in the early 21st century as the world began to go through a massive evolutionary leap.

Chronic viruses, as well as the above mentioned acute viruses, require special attention to the immune system with more rest and a healthy diet. This is how the body may enforce going within and allowing the space for a "LifeQuake Morphing Miracle" to take place.

These are real diseases. There is nothing psychosomatic about them. Real physical illnesses can manifest when it is time to change our lives and we refuse to listen to the soul's call. In my case, the stress of not listening to my body's mandate to slow down and turn within severely compromised my immune system, and blood tests indicated I had both Hashimoto's thyroiditis and Epstein-Barr Viremia.

Some people will bury their heads in the sand, yet this evolutionary process will be unrelenting. The soul will drag them through the muck and get their attention by whatever means necessary. Any illness that pulls the plug on your outer focus is tailor-made for a LifeQuake. Unless you embark on this inner journey when you become ill, your healing will be limited to treating the disease based on its physical symptoms, and you will miss the benefit of spiritual grace that is inherent to a Life-Quake.

Laura was an entrepreneur who ran focus groups. Her corporate clientele often required her to travel all over the country. Though she was diagnosed with cancer, once the surgery and radiation treatments were over, she went back to her usual rigorous pace—that is, until the cancer came back so perniciously that she had to undergo chemotherapy again. When she came to see me, she began to confront her fear of dying, stating that she already felt emotionally dead. Though she wanted to blame the chemotherapy for the numbness and isolation she felt, I encouraged her to go deeper. We worked with her dreams and uncovered significant parts of her that were clearly dying and needed to be released. One dream was particularly significant: she woke up on Christmas morning and saw a calico cat sitting under the tree, but the cat was dying. She brought the cat to a healer, who told her she needed to have it put down. At first, she refused. She did not want to let the cat die. We went back into the dream and allowed her imagination to show her what would happen if she did euthanize it.

She was terrified that if she ventured inside, it would mean leaving her career. I reassured her that stage two is not the time to make any drastic changes. It is a preparation period for the final severance of what needs to be released in stage three. If Laura had examined her life three years earlier, when stage two had originally descended, she may have put less stress on her immune system. She might have taken the time for reflection and discovered that the work she was doing was no longer authentic to her soul's purpose and made a change averting a physical crisis to get her attention.

The famous psychoanalyst Erich Fromm once said, "Man's main task in life is to give birth to himself." Some people get stuck in the birth canal; they keep moving back and forth between stages two, three, and four. They numb themselves out with avoidance tactics such as addictions, then hit the wall and go into therapy or treatment, but resist initiating any real change in their lives. This eventually leads to a dramatic loss of one kind or another.

The key to staying physically healthy during stage two is to listen to your body. It is vital to understand that it is slowing down for a reason. It requires a certain kind of metamorphosis now. Eat, drink, and exercise accordingly. Just as in stage one, notice how you feel after eating. As your immune system can be affected during this stage, it helps to get checked for food allergies. I loved, and still do love, bread of all kinds. I discovered that I was sensitive to wheat during my LifeQuake.

If you withdraw from eating foods you are sensitive or allergic to for a period of time, you may be able to return to them later without a problem. There are diagnostic tests that can help you determine what specific food sensitivities you have. Allergies are usually more obvious because they will cause you to break out in hives or cause a runny nose after eating them. As your body transforms, what you could easily eat before may no longer be right for you. It may be time to cut out caffeinated coffee and replace it with water-processed decaf or decaffeinated green tea. Instead of adding sugar or honey, try molasses or organic maple syrup. (Refined sugar taxes the immune system.) The key is to pay attention to your energy. This is a time when you really need to expend as little external energy as necessary. The anxiety that is triggered by the ego when your soul needs to withdraw from the world can tax your adrenals.

Seeing a Naturopath or holistic doctor who understands how to nourish rather than stimulate your adrenals and assist you in adopting a new diet is key.

Your exercise routine may also need to be reevaluated in this stage. Again, observe how you feel after your typical exercise routine. Are you fatigued or energized? If you are drained, cut back on either the duration or intensity of your exercise. You might also consider trying a new activity, as it might be time to shift gears altogether. Look into restorative yoga, Qi Gong, or Yoga Nidra. This non-strenuous practice strengthens and relaxes you with gentle, supported poses.

The shape of your body may go through a change. Grieve the loss of the body that was but don't despair, the seeds of your authentic self lay dormant under frozen soil. If you allow your body to slow down, spring will eventually come, and when it does, well-supported adrenals can mean weight loss if you had gained, and even more energy than you had before you entered your LifeQuake.

In seeking professional help, it's important to be clear about your needs. Query your health practitioner. Find out if he or she has a protocol to help you slow down. Acupuncture and certain Chinese herbs can support kidney/adrenal function in a gentle fashion. The Indian herb ashwagandha is also an adrenal tonic.

Another area of alternative medicine that addresses spiritual transformation and the emotional body is homeopathy. An accomplished classical homeopath will listen to your emotional symptoms and give you remedies that support this major life transition so that you can surrender your old life without fear, while strengthening your constitution in preparation for this transition.

Relationships

Not surprisingly, stage two can alter your relationships dramatically. As you continue to slow your pace, you may find a diminished desire for social activity. The wise person becomes very discriminating with his or her energy. If you're single or not involved with anyone, your temptation may be to blame your feelings of loneliness, isolation and emptiness on your marital status. If you're married or living with a partner, it may be tempting to believe the other person is to blame—you may believe that the problem is them; that you are just not turned on by him or her anymore.

In the realm of your personal relationships, you may feel like a robot. Your lack of sexual response could easily result in your looking outside of your primary relationship for gratification.

Tamiko had been married for five years when she began her secret affair with a fellow architect at her firm. She came to see me one year into the liaison. The proverbial bloom was off the rose. She no longer felt excited to see either her lover or her husband. Looking back, she admitted that the affair had originally put some zest back in her life; now, she found her energy dragging wherever she went. She had also started drinking too much wine at dinner in an attempt to buoy her spirits. Her husband, a psychologist, was concerned and suggested she see a therapist. As I assessed her LifeQuake questionnaire, I noticed that her answers suggested that she was yearning for a deeper spiritual life. She had been raised as a Buddhist and was Issei, first-generation Japanese. Therefore, her parents had huge expectations of her to follow a traditional Japanese spiritual life. When she went off to Harvard, she left the religion of her parents behind, embracing the cerebral, intellectual world of college life.

When Tamiko began working with me, she initially resisted any of the meditation techniques I gave her, fearful that it would pull her back into her religious upbringing. I assured her that quieting the mind was not part of any one religion but an essential need of the soul. However, her ego was seeking its spiritual food through her relationships with men. I instructed her to drop into her body with her breath and search for where the deadness felt most pronounced. She discovered that she felt pretty numb in her pelvic cavity. I observed that not only is this the area where sexual energy is stored but that it is also where the creative center can be for a woman. We began working on using her breath to unlock the energy in the second chakra that could be used to discover a spiritual source that comes from her feminine energy. She had been operating for so many years from her head that sex had become the only vehicle for her to feel her body.

Stage two of Tamiko's LifeQuake was dissolving the illusion that spiritual fulfillment could only come through sexual passion. She realized that searching for yet another man, now that she was withdrawing from her lover was a mistake that would ultimately take her down a dead-end street. Through the continual practice of sitting with her body and using the breath to surrender her defunctional style of intimacy, she was able to develop patience and mourn the death of an old self.

If you aren't married or in a romantic relationship, this is not the time to start dating.

More importantly, though, I want to repeat here that stage two is not the time to make any radical changes, the dying process itself takes time. If someone you love were given six months to live, you wouldn't declare him dead and move on as though he's already gone. You would choose to spend time with him and be as present to your grief and his transition as much as possible. Stage two of a LifeQuake is very much like this. The less you resist the death process of your old reality, the less painful it can be. If you keep breathing into your body where it is blocked or numb, a transformation will take place that allows you to enter stage three in a far less crisis-driven state.

Spirits—Not the Kind That Come in a Bottle

Regan worked as a barmaid in a fine restaurant at night. It was easy to just go through the motions of her job and sleep all day. She knew she wanted to find a career, but the money she was making in tips was too hard to give up. She had outgrown her circle of friends; they were all restaurant people who were more interested in partying after work than having a meaningful conversation.

Regan complained that she didn't have time to meditate, so I also suggested she sing the word "Om" in the shower while imagining the electromagnetic field around her body being cleansed with the water. You can do this any time by bringing your awareness to the top of your head, and with your inner eye, imagine light coming in through the top of your head cleansing your body as it moves all the way down to your toes. Take a deep breath into the solar plexus, and on the exhale, form the letter O with your lips, open your jaw, and allow the word "Om" to be spoken out loud for as long as your exhale lasts. Repeat this word thirteen times.

If meditation is not your cup of tea, there are other ways to experience stillness and enhance the development of the observer mind, your witness self. But let me just say this about meditation before we discuss alternatives: focusing on a word—a mantra—as you breathe in and out does two things. It develops a habit of directing the mind to one thought, to immersion with your spirit. In a time in which many adults are over-plugged into the virtual world, it is no wonder that so many of us refer to ourselves as ADD. Learning to calm the nervous system through conscious breathing can help with focus. People give up on meditation when they get bored or restless, not realizing that it's just like jogging or learning to play the piano. It takes a lot of practice, and to master it you must confront resistance in the first few months of forming this new habit. The other benefit of meditation is that you do begin to separate who you really are—your witness self—from your thoughts, even when you're not meditating. This carries over into your day. You will more readily notice negative thinking and change your thoughts more easily.

So if you decide to try meditation, start simple. Go back to the same word practiced in the chant mentioned above, "Om." There is a wonderful simplicity about that word. There are those who claim it is the primordial sound of the universe, and that all of humanity resonates to it. On the inhalation, think "Om"; on the exhalation, think "Om," and when your mind drifts, simply name it "thought," and go back to your breath and the mantra "Om." I suggest committing to six weeks of daily practice for ten minutes. If, at the end of six weeks, you don't see any results, then switch over to one of the following exercises.

For those of you who simply can't sit still, you can practice walking meditation. The walking meditation I suggest in this stage is to be very present to your surroundings. Start with your neighborhood. What do you notice in your body emotionally as you walk out onto the sidewalk, past your home? Continue to keep track of your feeling states as you observe parts of nature, such as trees and squirrels. How are these different from your feeling states as you observe passing cars and areas where there are buildings? If you are fortunate enough to live completely in nature, notice what interests you and where you have begun to go dead in your interest. Feel your body as it makes contact with the ground. Be as present to your surroundings as possible.

If you live in the city, you can do this meditation in your neighborhood or local park but whenever possible, go for a drive outside the city to a reserve or a place that allows you to connect with Mother Earth. Now observe your thoughts. Does anything change in your thinking after placing a focus on being present in your body and psyche first? I suggest doing this exercise also at a time of day when you can chant the "om" without feeling self-conscious that someone might be watching you. Do this for about the first ten minutes of the walk. If you live in the city and fear you'll be seen as a lunatic, chant for ten minutes before leaving the house. You will probably find yourself much more present and serene when you venture out the door. Now, set an intention to let go of all beliefs that no longer serve you.

Divine Coincidences

We discussed the concept of divine coincidence in chapter one, but let's review and take a look at its significance in stage two.

A divine coincidence is an event or experience placed in your life to assist you in moving in the right direction. Sometimes it happens because you are off course and your soul conspires with the universe (or if you prefer, God) to give you a sign. If you pay attention to unusual occurrences, stage two needn't feel quite so austere. If we are truly engaged with life as it unfolds around us, our souls can magnetize people, animals, and even angels (if you believe such helpers exist) to assist us on our journey.

Although many times, divine coincidences come in a seemingly unexpected fashion, they also can be called in. You can ask to be shown a sign to give you some direction. In fact, by consciously choosing to invoke it, you don't have to bring in a wake-up call that gives you the message in a harsh way. I'm sure you've heard it said that when the student is ready, the teacher appears. This is true for divine coincidences, too. When the receiver is ready, the message comes through. One uncanny coincidence can completely change your point of view and open all new vistas to you.

I hear stories of coincidences that are so unique and downright mystical, they almost look like carefully orchestrated divine interventions, specifically designed to bump us back on course when we've lost our way. A chance meeting between writer and columnist Michael Raysses and a complete stranger proved to be exactly that, a turning point that corrected his course.

Michael had been an actor for many years, achieving a modicum of success before falling on hard times. "I no longer felt any passion for acting," he remembered. For the first time in his professional life, he was forced to take a nine-to-five job. One morning while driving to work, he found himself feeling utterly lost. Desperately needing a cup of coffee, he decided to make a quick stop at a café. Before he could do so, he almost struck an elderly man in the crosswalk. He narrowly avoided hitting him and quickly pulled to the side of the road near the café.

As he took his place in line, he noticed the same elderly man standing in front of him. The old man greeted him, almost as if he was an old friend. "This caught me totally off guard," Michael remembered. Moved by the man's warmth, he interceded on his behalf when the old man found himself the victim of coffee house lingo. "He didn't know what the hell venti, grande, or tall meant," Michael reasoned. "So I stepped up and ordered for him."

Although he was running late for work, Michael inexplicably found himself asking the old man if he could join him for a moment on the café's patio. The elderly gentleman motioned to an empty chair, as if he had been expecting Michael the entire time.

The casual chat that followed held many gifts. His new friend was a Holocaust survivor who had come on hard times of his own. He had suffered a stroke and was estranged from his grown children. Coincidentally, he began talking about the very same things that had been haunting Michael that very morning. The more he talked, the more resigned the old man became. And, by the time he finished his story, he wasn't talking about the future anymore. "It was as if he had no future to speak of," Michael said.

The old man accepted Michael's offer of a ride to a cross-town bus stop. As he exited the car, he did something that Michael will never forget. "We were about to say good-bye, when he asked if he could tell me something. I said, 'Sure.' He took my hand and said, 'Michael, in your eyes I see a man who can do anything he wants!' Taken aback, Michael reflexively took his hand back. The old man then grabbed it with even more intensity, kissed it three times, and then vanished. Michael was speechless.

It was a while before the experience with the elderly gentleman finally reached his core. "I was really unhappy with things. I had been writing sporadically, but I was afraid to do it with any commitment. What if I failed? How would I be able to handle the inevitable rejection that being a writer involved, especially after years of struggling as an actor?" I asked Michael what he thought the old man had come to teach him. "Meeting him as I did, I think he was giving me a glimpse of a 'Christmas future,' so to speak. His disappointment with his life, his whole demeanor—he was exactly like old Mr. Scrooge. He woke me up and showed me that I didn't have to be a victim of 'Christmas past,' either."

Life provides us with synchronicities every day. Become attuned to them, and they will guide you along your way. Australian aboriginals entirely trust nature to speak to them in this way, and you can develop a relationship with the phenomenal world that is likewise reciprocal and informative. What you are really doing is opening your subconscious and intuitive mind. It's easy to close the windows of perception when you live in a city where the pace of life is full of frenzy. So I invite you to make a point of opening your attention and noticing little synchronicities that show you how, when, and where it's time to make a change. When these divine coincidences happen, take time to be still and ask within for deeper understanding.

Building Elements

In stage one we began developing the first set of building elements for our new foundation. To review, if we are approaching *The LifeQuake Repurposing Roadmap* consciously, those elements are keen observation and listening. We use our minds to observe life events and listen to our body for messages as to when and where a cycle is ending, as well as to what in our life is no longer growing in a positive direction.

In stage two, the building elements to develop are *detachment* and *acceptance*. After we master keen observation, we begin using the mind to detach our identity from the outside world. A gradual separation from tribal identity has begun. The emotional numbness or death process of stage two compels us to ask essential questions about who we are and what our purpose is. This happens while we are still entrenched in our former life. If we willingly detach from our dependence on outer substances to provide security and sense of self, we can gently transition and begin to accept that life as we've known it is ending. The process here in stage two is somewhat like the stages a person goes through in Elizabeth Kubler-Ross' book, *On Death and Dying*. The biggest distinction is that it is not another person who is dying. Your former self is the one being left behind, and yet the mourning process is very real. Your old identity is dying. You, who defines yourself in terms like, "I'm an accountant" ... "I'm Susie's mother" ... "I'm Daniel's wife" ... "I'm a Christian (or a Buddhist)" ... "I'm in AA."

Over time, the ability to detach brings a sense of spaciousness to your mind. In that openness, you begin to distinguish between thoughts that support your wellbeing and those that don't. In this way, you can begin to question the cultural programming and outdated beliefs that do not serve you.

The building element of acceptance goes hand in hand with the ability to be the watcher of your mind. It's almost a two-step dance—detach, accept, detach, accept, detach, accept. Some of the realities you will be challenged to accept are extremely painful while others are less so. For example, you have to accept that:

+ You can't seem to engage with your usual exuberance and vitality.

+ You need time alone and don't feel like socializing quite as much.

+ You feel "not yourself" for a time and uneasy with others.

+ You need more rest than usual.

+ What once made you happy now leaves you feeling flat.

+ Your biochemistry is shifting gears as your body is reconstructing.

This is not to say that you can't go through the letting-go process and experience happiness. Happiness comes from letting go of what was and sourcing your soul. A wonderful book about moving through difficult times and staying in touch with joy is *Happy for No Reason* by Marci Shimoff, the author who wrote the foreword to this book.

Many ancient spiritual texts speak of knowing when to sow and when to reap, when to expand and when to contract, when to move forward and make changes and when to retreat. It will be difficult, if not impossible, to master acceptance and detachment if you turn to artificial substances to get your mojo back. Doing so is like putting your old life on a respirator. Affairs, drugs, caffeine, even vitamin or herbal supplements are not going to breathe oxygen into a lifestyle or identity that is ready to die, if it's not already dead.

We often throw proverbial good money after bad before realizing that something needs to end or be eliminated. This is true of our personal lives, as well as our collective lives. Wars like Vietnam and Iraq have shown us this again and again.

To go back to the premise that we evolved from the earth, we are building an inner foundation that is earthquake proof: an inner foundation that adapts to change and is simultaneously unshakeable in its resolve and fluid in its function.

The Toolbox

The following tools will assist you in countering the tendency to hold on when it's time to let go and honoring the natural ending of cycles in your life.

Heaven and Hell

This exercise is a combination of both contemplation and writing, so have a notebook or journal handy, along with a pen. In this exercise, there is no judgment on your attachments. For the sake of using a metaphor that compares what is most conscious to what is most unconscious, we will look at our attachments as three tiers to suggest the psyche as layers. Make a simple graph labeling the tiers as follows from each part of the exercise.

After reading this exercise, begin by closing your eyes while seated in a comfortable chair. Take a moment to settle into your body through focused breathing. Now, think of the one thing that you are aware of being most attached to. It might be your job, your health, your partner, your home, etc. Imagine that it has been taken from you through whatever circumstances you can think of. Notice what you feel in your body and where you feel it. Breathe into it with long, slow breaths. Now allow yourself to experience a radiant violet light coming in through the top of your head, traveling all the way into where you are feeling the loss and pain. Keep open, while allowing this light to fill you. One by one, bring in the next thing or person to which you have the greatest attachment. Do the same process. Stay with this for ten minutes, if you can. When you open your eyes, list the people or things to which you have the greatest attachments in your graph of the first tier.

Now, the second tier is to think about addictions and beliefs to which you are attached. Imagine how you would feel if you gave up alcohol or sugar or prejudices you may have. For example, when I did this exercise, I located in my body my addiction to being special. What if there was nothing special about me? I allowed myself to feel the emotion connected to being ordinary. Imagine giving up your beliefs about being successful, spiritual, prosperous, etc. Go through a list in your mind of beliefs about yourself; now, imagine what your life would be like if each of those beliefs or habits were gone.

The last tier is to imagine giving up traits of the negative ego, such as self-criticism, shame, and self-loathing. What is your fear around giving them up? Take each one separately and experience yourself without it. Write about your experience as to how you feel in your body in their absence.

Developmental Steps to Change Mastery

✓ Become identified with the watcher of your thoughts, not your thoughts.

✓ Understand that life is cyclical and prepare in advance when a cycle is ending.

✓ Begin to acknowledge that nothing outside yourself will ultimately fulfill you.

✓ Consciously feel the dying process of your old life.

3

The Seismic Temblor: Radical Severance

Onset

Panic attacks. They must be panic attacks, I told myself, hoping to get a handle on what was happening inside me. The tremors always came at night, when I was lying still in bed or relaxing in front of the television. The sudden upheaval was not connected to a particular worry or thought. Something inside me just felt like it was shaking loose, as though the ground beneath me was moving. In its aftermath, it only made me tighten a death grip on my life. Because I had refused to go inward and face the fear, my soul was getting my attention the best way it knew how.

The Six-Day War

Over a period of six days, my ego and spirit clashed on the front lines of my consciousness. But this war's battlefield was on the streets and highways of Southern California. I'd had three car accidents in six days, and not one of them was seemingly my fault. The first accident occurred when I was concluding one of my shopping sprees, an expensive habit that had become quite frequent. Only a few minutes before, while trying on a beautiful red leather belt, I was taken aback by the vacant, half-dead gaze I saw in the mirror. Then, as I pulled out of South Coast Plaza, my treasured BMW was rear-ended. At first, I didn't even think about my injuries; my only concern was for my "beemer," its trunk now folded in like an accordion. Not until the next day, when I felt the after effects of whiplash, did it even occur to me that my body might also have been hurt by the impact.

My BMW went right to the body shop, and I went right back to business as usual in a rented Subaru. Two days later, I was approaching a major freeway interchange and traffic slowed suddenly. When the Subaru's brakes failed, I pumped the pedal and the car spun out of control. Eight lanes of traffic became like the Mad Teacup ride at Disneyland. For the first time in my life, I truly surrendered and in that moment, I became one with the steering wheel. When the car finally stopped, I was facing oncoming traffic, five lanes over. Miraculously, not a single car had been hit. Like the walls of the Red Sea, traffic had somehow parted to make a path for my brakeless vehicle to reach the side of the road. Shaken to the core, I decided that now might be a good time to stop driving for a while.

Two days later, my family arrived from out of town. It was my birthday, and we had planned an outing to the flea market in Newport. I appointed my brother Vince as the chauffeur. Climbing into yet another rental car, I intentionally chose the safest place in the car—the center position in the back seat. My mother was on one side of me, my godmother on the other. Surely, I would be safe now! About five miles up the freeway, traffic once again slowed down quite suddenly. My brother hit the brakes, and a massive, ebony-colored pickup truck plowed directly into the back of us. The driver was drunk. As I sat on the side of the road, holding the neck brace I'd been wearing since the first accident, my world began to unravel.

My Jungian analytic training had taught me to look at symbols. In each accident, the car had been pushed forward from behind. The message was clear: I would no longer be allowed to stay stuck. I had to move forward, like it or not.

To the outside world, my life looked great—successful practice, beautiful home in San Juan Capistrano, successful husband who adored me, and yet on the inside, so much was wrong. Where was I to begin?

After two months of hanging in limbo and going to physical therapy, I decided to attend an international transpersonal psychology conference at Asilomar. I accidentally walked into a workshop with Jacqueline Small before I realized that I was in the wrong room, but something inside me said "Stay." A pioneer in the field of addiction recovery, Small led us through an exercise that used music and visualization to heal the seven chakras in the etheric body. In that half-hour exercise, I started to wake up from the dream I had been living and began to follow my gut instincts. I came back from Asilomar and deconstructed my life. Over the next fourteen months, I left my practice, my husband, and the home we had shared for seven years. With no clue as to what I was going to do next, I continued to follow the messages I was receiving and moved to Los Angeles, terrified.

What It Appears to Be

Stage three begins when life as you've known it comes apart. In the immortal words of the late, great actress Bette Davis in the film *All About Eve*: "Fasten your seatbelts—it's going to be a bumpy night." This stage often looks and feels like a crisis. If we're still asleep and haven't begun to recognize the mandate for change, it might show up as a dramatic event. For example, you get laid off from your job, someone close to you dies, you get sick, and/or you experience the effects of a global disaster.

You're standing on shaky ground if you allow your attention to be completely consumed with the outer drama. It's easy to get pulled into your circumstances and identify them as the real problem when, in fact, the real problem is beneath the surface. On a practical level, the crisis du jour will likely have left you with a lot to attend to. There are things to fix, feelings to assuage, people to talk to, and decisions to make. In my first LifeQuake, there were three cars to repair, countless insurance forms, two months of physical therapy, a practice to sell, and a divorce to settle. With all of that going on, it's easy to miss the writing on the wall. If you're in a LifeQuake, there's a danger in making crisis management your sole focus. What's really important is the softer, wider focus that engages your intuition, so you can see the pattern and actually read what is written on the wall.

Everyone's process is different, of course. A LifeQuake need not lead to divorce, moving to a new location, or letting go of everything. Mine was more radical than some because there were wide chasms of faulty programs breaking open that had sealed off my soul's true yearnings.

As we've seen in the past two chapters, much of the action, the morphing process, happens internally. All of that is preparation for the very tangible change that takes place when you shed an identity that is no longer authentic. Prior to the shedding phase of stage three, radical changes are premature. If you've done the work of stage two, stage three is far easier because you can sever the ties that no longer serve you with clarity and full awareness.

For Martin Rutte, editor of *Chicken Soup for the Soul at Work* and author of *Project Heaven on Earth*, stage three began with fatigue. First, his enthusiasm for public speaking waned, and then he closed down his management-consulting business. With no trauma and no drama, he simply recognized he needed time off. Work wasn't fun anymore, so he simplified his life and made room for what he really needed—rest.

I observed this ability to move out of an old cycle without crisis in just a few of the people I interviewed. These people, Martin included, had three things in common: 1) although they didn't have a clue what was next, they did have absolute faith in themselves and/or a spiritual force that guides their lives; 2) they were less attached to material comforts and more willing to scale back their standard of living because they trusted their ability to recreate that abundance in a more authentic form; 3) they all maintained some kind of ongoing practice of meditation, contemplation, or prayer. In other words, they all had a secure inner foundation and therefore were better prepared to let go of a dying identity that was no longer viable.

What Really Is Happening

You might ask why you need to deconstruct your life to enter the next cycle. Why can't you keep your old life and just evolve your consciousness, right where you are? Let's look again at the analogy that my experience with car accidents offers, as it relates to what really is happening. "Braking" down my old life signaled the breakthrough that could only come once I stopped and listened to the inner promptings that were pointing in a new direction. The path ascribed by my old value system was a dead-end, and my soul knew it. My conscious mind fought to deny, repress, and ignore this knowledge because to know it was to question the very foundation on which I'd built my life—my house, my husband, and the worldly success I'd achieved. All of that had to be broken down and rebuilt on the bedrock of awareness and conscious choice.

Another potent metaphor for what really is going on is the timeless teaching story about pouring new wine into old skins. When you pour the new wine (awakened consciousness) into old skins (your former value system), they just burst. You must make a new skin (the witness) and then pour the new wine into it.

In chapter two, I discussed the journey that begins when we recognize the witness self who observes our thoughts. Remember that the ego mind is composed of all the layers of programmed beliefs that we have absorbed from the outer world. Our sense of who we are often comes from the outer life we've constructed.

In this stage, what's really happening is a radical severance from this outer shell of our identity. The severance causes any false or defunct structures on which we've built our life to shatter and fall apart. The old persona is disintegrating so that the authentic self can emerge. This is the essence of the Prigogine theory in quantum physics. In its most basic interpretation, the theory states that when an organism can no longer function in its current form, it bursts apart so that it may reconstruct at a higher level of functioning. In almost every ancient civilization there is a myth that analogizes this same phenomenon. In Greek mythology, the phoenix bird rises from the ashes, symbolizing immortality, resurrection, and life after death. Both the Greeks and the Egyptians associated the phoenix with the sun god.

According to the Greeks, the bird lives in Arabia near a cool well. Every morning at dawn, the sun god would stop his chariot to listen to the bird sing a beautiful song while it bathed in the well. Every 500 to 1,461 years the bird would sense that its death was near and would build a nest of aromatic wood. It would then set the nest on fire and be consumed by the flames. A new phoenix would spring forth from the pyre, embalm the ashes of its predecessor in an egg of myrrh, and fly with it to Heliopolis, "City of the Sun." There, the egg would be offered to the sun god and placed on his altar.

In Egypt, the phoenix was usually depicted as a heron, peacock, or an eagle. After three days, a resurrection would take place and the bird became the resurrected Osiris, god of the underworld and vegetation.

While chaos theory offers a scientific basis for this metamorphosis, the myth gives us much more by offering an image and an archetype. In the same way that a picture is worth a thousand words, an image by-passes our analytical mind and speaks directly to the soul. Archetypes, likewise, are the soul's language; they are universal patterns that can help us understand the paradox of our existence. The most profound message of this myth lies in the bird's ability to anticipate, prepare for, and then complete a cycle of growth. The bird builds the nest and then sets it afire; it doesn't wait until someone comes along to torch it. It doesn't wait until it has no more food. It knows instinctively when the time has come to die, and it knows, just as sure, that it will rise from the ashes into a new life.

All the myths of resurrection, from Sumeria to China, share a common time frame of three days. Wouldn't it be nice if we could recon-struct our life in three days, like a segment of a home-improvement reality show? Unfortunately, it often takes longer than that, although we slow the process down by holding on to outmoded beliefs and iden-tities, and that resistance can manifest dramatically to get our attention. However, if you become masterful at intuiting when to change your life before you are forced to, you become like Osiris, the Egyptian god of the underworld. The underworld represents the subconscious mind, and you can gain entry to it through dream work, various forms of psy-chotherapy, meditation, and for some, entheogenic drugs derived from plants such as ayahuasca and psilocybin mushrooms. Further, plant medicine is now being shown to have great efficacy in treating mood disorders in mainstream clinical trials.

When you venture into the part of your psyche that is subterranean or below conscious awareness, you can access unknown or disowned parts of you. These, in turn, often play an important role in new begin-nings.

Though this is the stage where it may feel like your life is falling apart, it's actually the beginning of it coming together in a new way. Like the phoenix bird, each time you journey through a LifeQuake con-sciously, the release into the fire of transformation occurs more rapidly. You learn to release your attachment to who you were and surrender to the unknown with less and less resistance. Here in this stage, you can no longer lie to yourself.

In previous chapters we looked at addictions as symptoms of resistance to the transition occurring through a LifeQuake. Addictions provide a convenient coping mechanism; they allow us to avoid the requisite burning, but they also delay the necessary and beneficial awakening of consciousness. If we become increasingly dependent on substances or people to manage this gap, our addictions may be the catalyst for major upheaval in stage three.

Relationship Addiction

Born to a Caucasian mother and an African-American father, Tara Moore grew up in the cross fire of racial prejudice and constant physical and emotional abuse. Her natural father, a musician, abandoned Tara when she was just a baby. Shortly thereafter, Tara's mother paired up with a wealthy Caucasian drug dealer, and the three moved into an all-white commune.

With San Francisco's music scene as a backdrop, Tara grew up with a mother and grandmother who pretended not to notice that she was half black. Tara was beaten repeatedly during childhood, until she finally fought back at age ten. And although the physical abuse stopped at that point, the verbal and emotional abuse continued. In addition, Tara's mother and her mother's boyfriend had frequent screaming fights, followed by intense make-up sex. This pattern became part of Tara's sexual identity—a string of men entered her life, each enacting the same dynamic that Tara had witnessed at home.

Tired of struggling to make ends meet on a retail salesclerk's pay, Tara eventually went to work as an exotic dancer. She made big money as a stripper, but the drug and party lifestyle that went along with it kept her running on empty. The turning point came when her ensuing anxiety attacks led to a nervous breakdown at the age of twenty-five.

Part of her recovery process involved taking workshops from Landmark Education, a seminar company dedicated to assisting people in having breakthroughs in their lives. Tara went back to her original passion: fashion. She began as a marketing rep and worked her way up to executive status. She earned more than she ever dreamed possible. That success under her belt, Tara felt a strong desire to help others. She began offering erotic-movement workshops that helped women heal their sexual issues and body distortions, and recover from relationship addictions. Tara is a woman who walks her talk; today, she relates to men of all backgrounds and race from an empowered, confident center.

If you find yourself picking this book up while in the traumatic after effects of addictive behavior, know that recovery is possible. Many roads lead to freedom, and while twelve-step programs are right for many people, other approaches can also assist you to evolve beyond addiction. Inpatient treatment is often appropriate for some in stage three, especially for those with chemical dependency or serious eating disorders. In my consulting work with various facilities, I have found that many of their clients come in at stage three and move into stage four during their stay.

Other options include working with a therapist or coach who is trained in addiction recovery. What matters most is reaching out to those who can see the bigger picture, who can help you to get perspective and not become consumed by the immediate crisis.

Cracking Open When You Think You're Cracking Up

Let's go back to the earth and look at her as a metaphor again. Your fear-based beliefs are the "faulty" layers of the foundation. The soul wafts up from the core, as vapors of awareness move through these fault lines into your higher consciousness. Pressure builds as the ego-based mind struggles to hold on to beliefs based in your outer identity. The cracks widen with this mounting pressure from the soul. More truth rises to the surface of the conscious mind. An inner earthquake erupts, sometimes in the form of anxiety attacks, and a crisis occurs. Your outer reality forces the tectonic plates to shift. Your mind and its self-concept break off. The bedrock of your essential self, infused with newly awakened soul force, rises up to meet you. Eventually you are standing on new ground. It just doesn't feel solid yet.

It is easy to see why this whole process finds people wondering if they are "cracking up," when, in reality, they are cracking open.

How many people have been institutionalized or heavily medicated in the face of this upheaval? When the soul's truth begins to emerge, the break between these two forces erupts so forcefully that this emergence of the authentic spirit is misinterpreted. Though one can appear to be crazy, what's truly happening is a spiritual emergence. Christina Grof's book, *Stormy Search for Self*, explains this phenomena in detail. I highly recommend it.

Some people need to go crazy in order to find themselves. Their belief system has to be shattered before they can discover who they really are. Unfortunately, the mental health system does not always recognize the deeper restructuring that is happening and may prescribe strong medications that suppress the experience.

Historically, among early tribes and aboriginal peoples, when an individual had a breakdown it was seen as a breakthrough; that person often became a healer, shaman, or prophet. He or she would leave the tribe and go into the forest or desert on an initiatory journey. They were believed to have left the ordinary world behind to connect with the nonordinary realm.

This world beyond the mundane could possess an individual for a long period of time. New information and insight could be brought to the tribe in this way.

In the mainstream of Western civilization, we have no such initiations. Most people don't have a place to go where their visions will be recognized as a call to new information; instead, they are diagnosed with a mental illness. Moreover, there is no place where they can rest and heal in seclusion and be tended to by professional healers who can help them integrate. Unless you work with a trans-personally oriented psychotherapist or psychiatrist who can distinguish this soul emergence from a psychotic break, medication will often be offered as a solution. As you can see from my repetition of this message here from chapter two, it's important to get into the hands of the right clinician while in a LifeQuake.

Healthy Upheaval

Some psychiatrists have broadened their perspective to a more holistic and less pathology-focused viewpoint. They are the exception, however, and not the rule, so it is up to you to ask the right questions. I interviewed one such doctor who practices an orthomolecular approach to the "cracking up/cracking open" phenomenon—the preeminent psychiatrist Dr. Hyla Cass. The author of several books, including *Natural Highs*, *Supplement Your Prescription*, and *The Addicted Brain and How to Break Free*, Cass advances a natural approach that can rebalance brain chemistry. She is one of a small number of psychiatrists with a transpersonal orientation who also looks at the spiritual roots of an emotional or physical breakdown and treats the person accordingly.

Any ignored health issues that began to emerge in the first two stages can reach catastrophic levels in stage three. If you are still consuming stimulants, such as sugar or caffeine, you will probably experience a marked increase in your anxiety levels. If anxiety does present, two chemicals in the brain become overstimulated—norepinephrine and cortisol. This causes the brain to shut down from the overload, which impairs one's decision making ability.

When the depression of stage two or the anxiety of stage three begins, specific supplements that may help, include vitamins, amino acids, and herbs. They can provide support for the neurotransmitters that will allow you to manage your symptoms as you employ the psycho-spiritual tools given in each chapter. Dr. Cass recommends paying attention to your nutritional needs during this time of crisis. She explains, "During times of stress, the raw materials needed to make neurotransmitters are diverted to support the stress-response system, leaving the brain and body depleted, and you, depressed, anxious, and sleepless. A balanced diet of high-quality protein, complex carbohydrates, and healthy fats (as in fatty fish), as well as nutritional supplements are vital to restoring physical balance and recovering emotional balance. Take extra vitamin C (4000 mg daily) to support the adrenals, and CBD oils without THC (also referred to as hemp oil) for anxiety can help some people. A great article on the impact this supplement can have on the immune system in a time of crisis can be found at **cassmd.com/can-cbd-improve-immunity**. Ginseng, rhodiola, kava, and, once again, ashwagandha help the body adapt to stress.

You will also need at least 500 mg of magnesium daily to calm your nervous system and relax your muscles. If you should find yourself in an emergency situation, like an auto accident or any other sudden trauma, there are two remedies you can buy at any health-food store: one is a Bach flower cure called Rescue Remedy and the other is a homeopathic remedy (200 Ck) called Arnica Montana. You may need some herbal help to sleep as well.

Prescription medications will only lead to dependency, while natural products actually supply the materials your brain and body need to calm down so you can enjoy deep, restorative sleep. Taking tryptophan at bedtime is often very helpful. You might also try calming amino acids such as theanine, taurine, and GABA."

All of these specific formulas support the system during times of stress; all are described by Dr. Cass on her website (**www.CassMD. com**). It provides a wealth of information on products, treatment options, and professional resources.

If a health crisis appears in stage three, it's important to work with both the appropriate medical doctors and a counselor of some sort so that the "dis-ease" in the body can lead to psycho-spiritual healing. Because the adrenals are often dramatically affected in stage three, the immune system may crash if you are resisting making changes.

Nothing that happens to you in this stage needs to become loss if you lean into it. Whatever you need to go through your LifeQuake and thrive can happen, if you allow things to fall apart so they can come together in a higher form.

If catastrophic loss is part of your LifeQuake, it's very important to embark on a therapy program that can release emotions from the tissue as soon as possible so that post-traumatic stress disorder (PTSD) does not progress from an acute to a chronic condition. The guided visualizations at the end of this chapter will assist this process, but I encourage anyone suffering from PTSD to find a therapist trained in eye movement desensitization and re-patterning (EMDR) or Somatic Experiencing. Learning "Tapping" (also called EFT) can also assist you in treating your own anxiety as a daily stress management tool. Nick Ortner, the founder of The Tapping Solution has lots of free videos on YouTube for dealing with anxiety in times of disaster or crisis. These short-term therapeutic techniques are highly effective for clearing trauma lodged in the body.

Workplace

We spend so much of our waking lives in our careers. It's no wonder that stage three can affect one's work and place of work dramatically, especially when we are caught unprepared. To return to the first collective crisis of this century, the 2001 attack on the World Trade Center is a dramatic example of a stage-three crisis at the global level that was meant to prepare us for the crises that would later unite us through climate change and pandemics. The 2001 attack on the World Trade Center is a dramatic example of a stage-three crisis at the collective level. One account from a 9/11 survivor struck me as a particularly graphic example of what is required of us in stage three. This man reported risking his life as he went floor by floor to warn others and help them get out of the burning building. He came upon one young woman, sitting at her desk; she was the receptionist on that particular floor. He yelled at her, "Get out! Get out now!" And she replied, "My boss told me not to leave this desk until my break."

What this story highlights is our ingrained tendency to hold tight to the old rules and external authority when the world as we know it turns upside-down. I'm not here to judge anyone's response to extreme crisis; we all have our version of staying glued to our desk. I knew for some time that my workplace, a medical building wasn't quite right. I'd wanted to do healing work in a quiet space. My training had always emphasized the importance of having a neutral space; it was considered unprofessional to see patients in one's home. My inner voice said otherwise, but I ignored it. Then the doctor who had sublet me a part-time office said he wanted to rent the space out full-time, giving me twenty-four hours' notice to vacate. I had clients scheduled that very week, and with no time to find another location, I decided to see them in my living room. One by one, they expressed how much more peaceful they felt seeing me in that nonprofessional environment.

In both examples above, holding onto a desk or holding on to a professional image, each of us was really afraid to let go of "the rules." We had both been deeply conditioned to believe that playing by the rules leads to success—or at least leads to freedom from reprimand. It's fear that keeps us wedded to this idea that security comes from playing by the rules. When a crisis hits, you can't afford to stay locked on a fixed idea of what will provide safety, because this narrows your choices.

Had I insisted upon maintaining a professional image, I never would've discovered how much more at ease my clients were when they came for sessions in my home. Years later, that ease would be extended to working with clients over the phone so they were in their own homes. Now since the latest pandemic, many people have restructured their lives to home-based workplaces.

The best way to prepare yourself to meet any crisis is to create a mobile, adaptive foundation in your psyche. Develop the building elements in each stage, and you'll be able to meet change with an open mind, giving you a broader range of choices.

Apply the building elements in your workplace. Examine both the place you work and your work habits for their effect on your health and well being. Ask yourself these three questions:

+ Do I like my job?

+ Do I like the people I work with, including my boss?

+ Is my work environment a healthy one that supports my overall wellbeing?

If you answered no to one of these, eventually you must begin to plan your next move. If you answered no to all of these questions and you have no exit plan, chances are high that you'll encounter a dramatic event that forces your transition. Statistics show that people with the "golden handcuffs syndrome," who stay in a job for the benefits, take more sick days per year than those who report high job satisfaction.

It is also important to get as much rest as possible during stage three. Take a short nap in the afternoon, even if it means going out to your car if you work away from home. At one point during my first LifeQuake, I took a nine-to-five consulting job that required me to work in an office. I made a habit of taking twenty minutes out of my lunch break to retreat to the parking lot. Whether for a quiet meditation or a quick nap, those few minutes made a huge difference in my afternoon performance.

Resting the body midday actually prevents you from going to bed in that tired/wired state that can lead to insomnia. If insomnia becomes a problem, in spite of the protocol given above from Dr. Cass, one or two sessions with a hypnotherapist can be very effective. If you're unable to find one in your area, a sleep-induction recording might work just as well. There are guided visualizations on my audio recording *The LifeQuake Repurposing Method* found on my website as well: **LifeQuake.com.**

A friend and colleague shared how the radical severance of an old identity led her into a healthier experience of transfunctional adulthood.

Joanna had been working in a lucrative sales position when she found herself feeling increasingly dissatisfied with her job. A former actress, she missed the magic of being involved in a repertory theater group. She decided to enroll in an acting class in the hope of recapturing some of the creativity and camaraderie she had so cherished when she was acting. And while acting no longer inspired the muse, one particular aspect of the acting classes did—working with an acting partner to delve deep into the subconscious mind. Though Joanna took several years to make the transition from her sales job into being a hypnotherapist, that time was full of enthusiasm and purpose. Her day job no longer bored her to tears. The office became a place where she could do two things at once: fulfill her responsibility to her existing customer accounts and move in the new direction at a relaxed, organic pace. For the first time in years, she felt enthusiastic about going to the office.

When I asked Joanna why she didn't have to hit the wall in order to realize it was time to change careers, she gave me a two-part response. First, she had faith that she would make money in her new career because she'd done well in previous endeavors. And second, she'd been a practicing Buddhist for many years, so her ability to observe her thoughts as separate from her true self was well developed. Buddhism had led her on a path of nonattachment, so she was comfortable with foregoing her previously abundant lifestyle for a period of time.

Joanna's LifeQuake is a good example of a transition that takes place easily when foresight, faith, and a disciplined spiritual practice are part of the equation. Pay attention to the message in your dissatisfaction before your life starts to deteriorate.

Lifestyle

Conventional wisdom would have it that the more complex a person's outer life is, the more difficult it will be to change. A person who has children, aging parents, and a mortgage to pay may feel he or she has fewer options than people without these responsibilities. However, when approached consciously, the most important radical severance that takes place in stage three is from "thinking inside the box." When you separate your sense of self from the outer life you've constructed and are clear about what you truly value, this detachment allows your conscious mind to tap into a universal consciousness where unlimited possibilities exist. The thing that dogs us in this phase of deconstruction is our subconscious mind. If our subconscious mind is still fear-based and attached to beliefs that our security comes from a certain lifestyle, all the wake-up calls, divine coincidences, and even physical symptoms will be ignored until the rug is pulled out from under us. Funny how people can believe that they have to stay in a job they hate to support their family—until they've been laid out by a heart attack. Somehow, when forced to, a family can learn to live more simply.

When I presented a workshop at a conference for teachers in Canada, a participant approached me afterward with his story. He'd been an ironworker and wanted to return to school and become a teacher but felt he couldn't because of his financial obligations to his wife and family. Then he sustained an injury to his hands and had to undergo surgery. During his recuperation at home, he began reflecting on his life. He was turning forty and recognized that if he really wanted to realize his dream, there was no time to waste. He began taking classes at night while caring for the children during the day. The family moved into a smaller house in a neighborhood with good schools, which saved the expense of private school. He and his wife both decided to forego buying a new car, as they were accustomed to doing every couple years. These two small concessions spelled big benefits to the overall well-being of the entire family.

If you cultivate a mind that thinks outside the box, you don't have to lose everything to make even a major transition. Remember, your career, relationships, community, and health practices only need to change in accordance with what your soul needs to move into transfunctional adulthood.

To reiterate, transfunctionality is a consciousness that is ultimately free of making automatic choices based on old programmed beliefs. This is a way of being that works with all three levels of what we call "mind." It uses the conscious mind to recognize and clear emotional blockages in the subconscious mind that are located in the body. It also taps into the universal mind through guided imagery or meditation.

Some people are so naturally plugged into their super-conscious mind that they can naturally access this unlimited universal intelligence. However, for most of us, when we feel that our security is threatened, we find it difficult to reach this plane. It is, therefore, critical to clear the fears or panic coming from the subconscious first, before attempting to access the super-conscious mind. In the Toolbox section, you'll be given some exercises to support your developing an agile mind that can move through the unconscious and the super-conscious mind more easily.

Relationships

Sudden upheaval in one's intimate relationships can often be a catalyst for stage three. Consider what happened to Robin, a housewife and mother of two, when the ground beneath her feet began to shake. It started with a call from a woman who claimed she'd had a child with Robin's husband. The child was eight years old, and the woman had been receiving child support since his birth. That would register an eight on any woman's emotional Richter scale.

Robin had been unhappy in her marriage for quite some time. Despite having acquired a graduate degree during the marriage, she'd been unable to motivate herself to go back to work. Her protracted stage two had included a bout with cervical cancer that was quite symbolic when looked at through the lens of energy medicine. She'd missed the wake-up call that had come five years earlier, when an anonymous caller told her that her husband was not away on a business trip in New York but was a few hours away at a hotel with another woman.

This time, however, the alarm bell penetrated her consciousness—the news about her husband's illegitimate child marked a turning point for Robin. As the youngest child in a large family, she'd been given messages from her father that she was incapable of handling financial responsibility, so she'd left it all to her husband. Her divorce became her initiation into spiritual adulthood. She hired and fired several male attorneys and in so doing, developed immunity to her need for men's approval. Moreover, part of her healing involved surrendering her Catholic style of praying to a male image of God in exchange for a non-gendered, spiritually mature co-partnership with universal consciousness. As we did the divine blueprint re-patterning meditation (see the Toolbox section), she felt a light coming through her body and a healing from all the bitterness she'd felt for her husband. Working with this exercise daily led her to begin a new career as a professional speaker.

For one of my clients, stage three began when he could no longer deny his sexual preference for men. Joe, a working actor with a secure job on a popular soap opera, feared that coming out would cost him his career. He became increasingly depressed by living with his girlfriend in a self-created closet, built on the idea that he could pass as a straight guy, if he just kept trying. As his depression deepened, he began to have panic attacks and decompensate while on set. In time, he was fired; the radical severance then began in earnest. Fortunately, a bit of residual income from a national commercial spot kept him afloat through stage three and into stage four. His first authentic choice was to attend massage school, a decision that allowed him to get in touch with his body. Joe met his soul mate, Al, a short time later; left his girlfriend and his acting career; and came out to his Midwestern Italian parents. He moved in with Al and began a private practice in massage therapy. Fifteen years later, Al and Joe are still together but Joe transitioned once again from a successful bodywork practice to becoming a Yoga Nidra teacher and now teaches all over the world through Zoom.

As I was writing this chapter, my South American housekeeper, Dianna, told me a chilling LifeQuake story. She was living in Brooklyn when the building her family lived in caught fire. Her whole family was forced to jump out the window in order to escape the flames. She and Nina, her identical twin, were the last in line to go out the window, but her twin freaked out when she looked down at the ground. Dianna convinced her sister that she would do the jumping; all Nina needed to do was climb on her back. Nina climbed on, piggyback style, but then suddenly pulled back from Dianna right before she jumped. The little girl's charred body was found in the closet, where she often went to find solace from a large family living in cramped quarters.

Death of a twin such as this is particularly traumatic for the surviving twin. In LifeQuake terms, the reconstruction phase will be deeply affected by a profound and irretrievable loss. What this traumatic experience taught Dianna was to never let fear of the unknown run her life. As horrific a loss as this was, to this day she holds the experience as a gift from her sister, a lesson on never letting fear run her life.

Life is tenuous. This stage prepares you for the moment when you may be required to walk away from everything you know. We've all heard the predictions and the threats such as climate change is accelerating, our economy is in peril, terrorism continues, and Artificial Intelligence may replace us. This is our shared reality, and anyone of us may be confronted with it during our lives. Have you stopped to think how would you respond if you woke up tomorrow and heard someone say, "Get out of your house today!"? How would you respond? Think about it. What if you had to walk away from all your worldly possessions? What if you had to do that in a matter of minutes? Would you be able to do it? If you were about to get on a plane, and you heard a small voice from inside you say, "Don't get on that plane. Wait for the next one," would you listen? What if you were about to get on the freeway, and you got an uneasy feeling about taking your usual route? Would you listen?

For Luciano Copete, the journey from being a corporate executive to owning his own international design firm (devoted to getting out the message of nonprofit organizations) did not require massive crisis. He remembers a pivotal experience that led to his giving up control over his life.

"I was twenty-five years old. I had conquered hotel management, had become a wine connoisseur for the top company in South Florida, had the perfect woman in my life, and was about to buy a condo in Coral Gables on the twentieth floor in the premier development in that area. I stood to make a $70,000 profit right away on this if I sold it. And then, it was a chance meeting with a man who had walked away from a very powerful position with Ford that changed my life. He invited me to a fire ceremony on the beach. At first, I thought, *"Oh, this is going to be a bunch of spiritual hippies hanging out."* When I arrived, I noticed that none of these people were drinking or smoking pot. There was a reverence about this ceremony that they were about to engage in. I was still in my corporate-suit mentality. As I changed from my jacket and tie to jeans and a T-shirt, an internal shift occurred.

Although this was a radical thing for me to do, strangely, I felt comfortable to be there. Then, the shaman leading the group mentioned that he came from Sierra Nevada, in the mountains of Colombia. I then got very interested because what are the odds of someone from this remote city I was born in to be here on the beach in Miami? He did a prayer with us in which we asked Mother Earth to show us direction for our lives. He then announced that someone in this group had a tremendous power that he had not unleashed yet. Well, I knew I had to talk to him. He told me that I was hiding my true power behind a "fake dress." I told him about the apartment I was going to buy the next day, and he told me to walk away. When I woke up the next morning, something told me he was right, so I backed out of buying the condo and put the down payment into my design business. For six months I questioned whether I had done the right thing. And then a huge hurricane came and hit South Florida, and this beautiful apartment complex was wiped out. It was then that I began to really surrender to my instinctual nature instead of my head," he recalls.

He elaborates," What I learned, over and over again, was that if you surrender yourself to your gut instincts, it will allow you to leap over the cliff. The key is to jump—but to jump after listening and surrendering to your body and where the energy is pulling you."

When a national or global catastrophe happens, and you see how others are being affected on the news, you can extract benefit from other people's responses by walking yourself through the experience in your mind as to how you want to respond if you are next.What would you do? Most of us just go into fear and hope it never happens to us. Further, set an intention that you now can intuit handling a catastrophe resiliently in advance, so you don't have to be as traumatized, when it hits your town, workplace, or home. I lived in an earthquake-prone city for many years. I would go through in my mind a behavioral rehearsal of what I would do if a major catastrophe hit, so that I would remain calm. As someone who does rely on her body instincts, I felt the earthquake, 9/11, and the global pandemic of 2020 months in advance. I didn't know what was coming, but I spent a lot of time in meditation on those days so that I could help others not to panic.

If you are reading this in the midst of a major crisis in your life, surrounding yourself with people who support and encourage you in such emotionally charged times is critical to moving through this stage more easily. If your mate or closest friends have traditional attitudes about security and are caught up in their own fears, reach out to one of the many groups that embrace a more expansive philosophy. Non-traditional examples include AA and other anonymous programs, the Unity Church, Center for Spiritual Living, MSIA.org, and Siddha Yoga meditation. Thankfully, since the latest global crisis, all are now available online to share with others around the world live. Also, if you belong to a church, reach out to your minister or parish priest for guidance.

Body/Spirit Practices

Sometimes even the most experienced people who meditate find it difficult to still their mind in stage three. If you find that to be true, there are four spiritual/physical disciplines that I recommend (also briefly suggested in stage 2): Hatha yoga, Qigong, Tai Chi and Yoga Nidra.

Everyone in the Western world is now familiar with yoga. Many people are unaware that there are many different types of yoga that do not involve physical movement as the specific practice. For example, Bhakti yoga is the practice of love and devotion; Karma yoga is the spiritual practice of selfless work; and Jnana yoga is the practice of seeking knowledge and discernment. The physical discipline most people are familiar with is called Hatha yoga. The ultimate purpose of all forms of yoga is the union of the individual soul with the universal soul. If you're practicing Hatha yoga during stage three, be sure to include a spiritual intention along with the usual desire to get the poses just right.

If you're interested in the philosophy that encompasses the principles and goals of yoga, read the Upanisads or the Bhagavad Gita.

While yoga originated in India, Tai Chi comes from China. Generally promoted as a moving meditation that is practiced to support health and longevity, Tai Chi Ch'üan (its proper name) is a soft-style martial art. Applied with complete relaxation, or "softness," in the musculature, its theory and application are quite different from that of the hard martial art styles, such as karate and tae kwon do.

Traditional Tai Chi training is intended to teach awareness of one's own balance and what affects it, awareness of the same in others, an appreciation of the practical value in one's ability to moderate extremes of behavior and attitude at both mental and physical levels. Studies have shown its effectiveness in children who struggle with attention deficit disorder.

Qigong (pronounced Chee Gong) means breath or gas in Mandarin Chinese; it also refers to the energy we produce by breathing; gong means work or technique. Generally speaking, qigong grew from the traditional Chinese view of the body and, specifically, from the understanding that our physical body has an energy field around it that is generated and maintained by the natural respiration or "qi" of the body. Qigong then is "breath work," or the art of managing the breath to achieve and maintain good health and, especially in the martial arts, to enhance the energy mobilization and stamina of the body in coordination with the physical process of respiration. Originally developed by Chinese warriors to create a repellant force field around the body, its modern use is as a potent means of keeping the body vital and strong.

Western practitioners of Qigong generally see it as a set of exercises, using the breath and subtle movement that regulate the energy of organ functions. It has many other benefits, including grounding one's body, mind, and spirit and enhancing complete stillness.

The underlying philosophy of all these Eastern disciplines is to achieve balance by harmonizing yin and yang, to gain mastery over the inner world (mind and emotions), and eliminate unnecessary suffering in the outer world. Each of the methods discussed above employs a deep focus on the body and the breath to accomplish this. When practiced daily, these disciplines can reduce anxiety, lessen the resistance to change you may be experiencing, and enhance the necessary detachment, thus allowing you to move through this time of radical severance.

If you incurred an injury that precludes doing any of the above energy practices, when you feel the overload of anxiety, one thing that everyone can do is go outside if it is daylight and look around you and breathe. Being outside opens the mind from a myopic state and if you can walk or get into nature, even better. If anxiety hits at night, get out of bed, put your headset on to your favorite music in another room, and shake your body. If all you can do is stand, feel the music and your anxiety, but have the intention of shaking it off the way animals do when they experience trauma. You can't hold the anxiety at the same time you are shaking and listening to music that brings you joy.

Divine Coincidences

In chapters one and two, the concept of divine coincidence was introduced as synchronistic events meant to guide you as you prepare for a life change. In the early days of stage three, divine coincidences can look like wake-up calls that warn you that the proverbial light at the end of the tunnel is an oncoming train.

One of my clients, a mother of two and a cocaine user, had a husband who was away on business most of the time. It was clear that her cocaine use was beginning to take too high a toll. Whereas once it had given her the energy she needed to care for toddlers, 24/7, now it depressed her. Although well aware of this, she was caught in the addictive cycle and couldn't stop. Then one day, just as she was about to call her dealer for another gram of coke, she got a call from an old friend and learned that a mutual friend had recently died of an overdose. The right information at the right moment—that's all it takes for a divine coincidence. Instead of one more dive into her addiction, she followed my advice and went to a Cocaine Anonymous meeting that very afternoon.

The key to finding opportunity in the most devastating losses is to shift your emotional gears. Rather than downshift into perpetual grief and loss, begin looking for clues and divine coincidences—new opportunities and unimagined good fortune can come into your life when you seize the moment.

Building Elements

The main building element at this stage is *surrender*. If you are practicing the building elements of the previous stages—*keen observation, listening, acceptance,* and *detachment*—you can do this, even in the face of major crisis. As you are able to surrender one life for the uncertainty of another, the labor pains are less intense and the onset of stage four is accelerated.

Don't worry if you started this book while in the midst of stage three of your LifeQuake. You can still read the first two chapters and assemble the building elements of stage one and two into your new foundation. I would also recommend re-reading the Toolbox sections in the earlier chapters and get started right away. The knowledge of how and when to surrender is built on the previous elements.

With each sudden crisis that I confronted, I was forced to surrender my attachment to my material life with greater and greater speed. When I was 28, it took me seven months to leave my home and marriage and another year to give up my profession and community. By age 42, when I was given two hours to walk out of my mold-infested home, I had so many lessons in detachment under my belt that I had no resistance when I walked out the door. I left everything behind, including treasured works of art, irreplaceable family photographs, and a collection of rare books. The ability to surrender is often born out of experience. When you've paid the high price of denial once, you'll be less likely to hold on to what is now defunct. This is just one of many levels of meaning behind the twelve-step slogan "Live and learn."

The Toolbox

By now, you've begun to build a new pattern of awareness as emotions arise. Even if you feel a lack of mastery, the key is awareness. If you've practiced the tools from stages one and two, you have a new way of dealing with boredom and numbness, by observing it without judgment. Now in stage three, your outer world is crumbling. Here, we must address major life change and the fear it evokes.

The following exercise focuses on the brain and central nervous system. This is where you begin to change your psychic and physical blueprint and maximize your ability to make lucid decisions in the midst of widespread upheaval.

This process is designed to begin the course of reconstructing your cellular memory. When repeated daily, it releases fear-based coping mechanisms at a vibrational level that then re-patterns the nervous system, so that adapting to change becomes easier. Eventually, you'll be relieved of the specific fear of change that can paralyze your will and narrow your focus, making it difficult to respond in your best interest. You'll learn to surrender to life from the present moment, while embracing an attitude of healthy expectation about change.

Divine Blueprint Re-patterning Meditation

(This exercise is on *The LifeQuake Repurposing Method* audio recording as well.)

Read the exercise in its entirety. Sit or lie down comfortably in a position that supports your entire body. If you're on the floor, put pillows under your knees. If you're sitting, make sure your back is supported and your feet are touching the floor. Now close your eyes. Breathe in to the count of five, and then out to the count of five. With each breath you take, feel yourself becoming more deeply relaxed. Once again, breathe in and breathe out. Now allow your awareness to move to the top of your head. Begin to experience "a column of golden light," your radiant light energy entering the top of your head. This begins the recognition of who you are when you are in your full potential self—your Wholy Self. With each breath you take, make the intention of allowing this light to enter into your brain. Continue breathing in and breathing out. As you breathe in now, allow your entire brain to be bathed in this light.

If you find it easy to visualize, see it gently entering into the top of your head and permeating the entire circumference of your brain. If visual imagery doesn't come readily for you, simply allow for a feeling to emerge (like a gentle tingling sensation) as light enters into your crown chakra and surrounds your head. This divine light is imprinting a new pattern into the neural pathways of your brain. Now, allow this light to expand and spread through your entire nervous system. You don't have to know how to do this. Just breathe it in with your intention.

Now, breathe the light deeply into the front of your head; relax your temples and forehead. As you breathe in and breathe out, your body goes even deeper into relaxation. Moving now to your jaw, allow the light to permeate and embrace your jaw, relaxing it. Keep focusing your breath into each body part, allowing for a gentle softening and release. Now move to your neck and your shoulders. Feel them release as you go deeper … deeper into relaxation. With each breath you take, this light, this radiant healing light, releases all tension, replacing it with a deep sense of harmony and balance.

Now move to your chest. Allow this radiant light to move into your lungs. Breathe in and breathe out. Now move into your heart. Experience your heart surrounded and filled with the light. And as you continue to breathe in the light, your heart takes in even more healing. And as your heart takes in the light, set the intention that your innate divine intelligence is transforming every cell of your body, activating a new level of trust of the unknown. All previous fear based beliefs with regard to change have been re-patterned. Repeat the following: "It is now safe to change. When I make the changes that are authentic, I always win. I can trust myself to move forward into the unknown." Return your focus to your heart and ask to be shown a symbol that represents an answer to any question you have about making changes now. When the symbol appears, ask to be shown its message. What is the next step to take?

Now, take another extra deep breath into your heart. You're now releasing the structure of your old life with positive expectancy. A new behavioral groove is developing. Throughout the day ahead, at the moment you experience fear, you can automatically take a long, deep breath, relaxing your body. You can now ask for guidance from the Wholy Self;

you listen to the message and then act in accordance with its wisdom. If you don't hear anything, set the intention that the answer will come spontaneously at some other time. Just know that you are now imprinted with this new pattern as you deal with crisis.

Now bring your awareness back to your heart, placing both hands over your heart. This is your anchor. We are now anchoring the building element of *surrender* into the heart. From now on, when you place your hands over your heart, it will center you and allow you to use your breath to soften and receive. This is at the core of the building element of *surrender*. You now release the structure of your old life with trust.

With daily practice, this will allow you to adapt more easily and effortlessly to both expected and unexpected change. You now make changes and resolve conflicts much more rapidly because you are in the flow. As crises present themselves, you now access solutions through a nervous system that has been programmed for adaptability. You respond with humor and lightness to what would have once triggered fear of loss. You're now spreading this light to every person you meet. At the end of the day, experience yourself feeling more balanced. Though you may be a little tired, you're no longer exhausted, because you're content with your success at *how* you did this day.

Now, allow the light that is you to expand, and with your intention, send it out to the planet. You can close with this affirmation: "I am now at peace. I am now in deep gratitude. I experience the world as the same. And so it is done."

Doing this exercise daily is an opportunity to clear old beliefs anchored in fear of change so that you learn how to adapt more quickly to change. A new pattern is then anchored so that chaos is experienced like labor pains. By surrendering to uncertain change and staying with it, you will enter each new cycle with less resistance and greater adaptability.

Developmental Steps to Change Mastery

✓ Transform your beliefs that crisis means loss or failure into a new definition of success that requires a natural organic de-structuring of outmoded forms.

✓ Breathe through the fear in your body when resistance to change occurs.

✓ Move forward before change becomes catastrophic.

4

The Cosmic Barbecue: Ego on a Spit

||||||||||||||||||||||||||||||||||||||||||||||||||||||||||||||||||||||||||||||||||||||||||||||||||||||||||||||

We fear to know the fearsome and unsavory aspects of ourselves, but we fear even more to know the godlike in ourselves.

~ Abraham Maslow

||||||||||||||||||||||||||||||||||||||||||||||||||||||||||||||||||||||||||||||||||||||||||||||||||||||||||||||

Imagine that you've been invited to a party in the desert. You don't have a precise map to get you there, just some general directions. You drive out of the city, full of anticipation. After some time, the road gets narrower and narrower. Eventually, you come to the end of the pavement. You've been told this is going to be a great party, and because you're feeling adventurous, you continue down the dirt road. Finally, at the end of the road you see a cluster of adobe bungalows that look abandoned. You get out of the car, feeling suspicious. Out of nowhere, an old man with a white beard appears. He points to a huge grilling spit with your name on it stretched across a dark hole. Suddenly, the phrase "Dinner is served" takes on a whole new meaning.

Ego on a Spit

This is the Cosmic Barbecue. This stage reveals the patterns and beliefs that have kept you from living authentically. By the time it's complete, you'll have shed the old identity that no longer suits you. In stage four, the fire of your soul blazes through all that is false, purifying your ego, making you lighter in the process. Resistance is not only futile, but it's also potentially painful. Surrender, the building element you learned at stage three, is your saving grace now. What lies within this dark night is the remarkable adventure of discovering your passion, your new soul purpose but it requires a deep excavation first.

Onset

Stage four involves a radical departure from the conventional mindset that governed your prior life. You've come to the end of that road. You may feel alienated from everything around you. The desert metaphor is a powerful and accurate one, used by poets and shamans throughout time to describe this stage of initiation into spiritual adulthood. Loneliness is the hallmark emotion of this stage.

What It Appears to Be

The feeling that you are apart from the world, abandoned by life, by God, and by the fates is precisely what roasts your ego. In stage four, your relationship with the familiar forms of your previous life dissolves. Everything you thought you knew or understood no longer holds water, and you thirst for a deeper truth than that which you've known before. At times, you may even feel desperate. Nothing that quenched that thirst in the past will do. This limbo place between who you were and who you are becoming is more than a little daunting. At least in stage two you had one foot firmly planted in the old reality. In stage three, your energy was focused on the fallout of the crisis or conscious, radical severance of your old life and handling the details of letting it go. In stage four, no outer compass can help you get your bearings. Try as you might to use old maps to find your way, they'll lead nowhere.

What Is Really Going On

In stage four, your soul exerts its full thrust, disconnecting everything outside you. This severance is purposeful, as it makes way for your journey inward. Being in the unknown without your past identity may initially feel uncomfortable, but it is where you can become free of the limitations from what you perceived was possible for you in this life. It is the place where pure potential exists and once you get comfortable with the lack of identity and connection to the outer world in the old way, miracles can happen.

Even if you maintain parts of your old life, you'll still feel alien and barren. What was once comfortable and familiar now feels foreign. Up until now, you've had a host of safe distractions to keep you from turning within. Now, even those distractions lend little comfort. Whatever structure you've managed to spare in your life won't save you from confronting aspects of yourself that you've denied. Carl Jung referred to this as the Shadow; I call this archetype the Cellar. Within the Cellar are disowned aspects of yourself that are suppressed in your subconscious mind. Although they contain further keys to making changes with greater adaptability; more specifically, they hold the key to your soul's calling.

I call these disowned sub-personalities our *Cellar Selves*. What they all have in common is shame—that's why they're in the cellar; we're afraid of them. We fear that by acknowledging them, we'll lose something that represents safety and security. For example, if you identify with being sweet and kind, one of your Cellar Selves may be a tyrant. Though recognizing the tyrant may be the key to claiming your power, you may fear what getting in touch with that part will lead to. For instance, you might very well know that the tyrant in you is capable of telling people off and in fact would love nothing more than to light into your boss. What we fail to realize, though, is that these hidden faces are like vintage wine—if stored too long in the cellar, they become sour. We need to open them up and enjoy their spirit.

For whatever reason, you've been hiding desires and personality traits you deem undesirable or threatening. The cast-iron door that kept them sealed away has now blasted open. Often it's the parts we've been denying that lead to our greatest realization. The desert is the perfect terrain in which to let these parts out of the cellar and into the light of day, where you can stop judging them as "bad." By claiming the sub-personalities contained in your cellar, you move from a polarized consciousness of "good me versus bad me" into feeling more integrated, more whole. Embracing disowned parts allows your subconscious mind to release this toxic shame and embrace your humanity, which can also make you a much more interesting character! What emerges through this fire is your Wholy Self. Noted writer Jalaja Bonheim speaks of this process in her book *Aphrodite's Daughters*: "Paradoxically, we achieve true wholeness only by embracing our fragility and sometimes, our brokenness. Wholeness is a natural radiance of love, and love demands that we allow the destruction of our old self for the sake of the new."

The Cosmic Barbecue may feel for some as if it's happening in slow motion. For others, it feels like a free-fall into the unknown. Whatever form it takes, it is always disorienting. But this very confusion compels you to sink deeper and deeper into your real self—the self you could not come to know until you went alone into the desert. Reflexively, you struggle to grasp something—anything—that will save you, define you, or put your feet on solid ground.

Your experiences in stage four combine the disowned and undeveloped Cellar Selves into your conscious personality, paving the way for your transfunctional self to emerge. The defunct parts of your old life are stripped away, freeing your spirit. You'll also learn numerous ways to summon, own, and activate these Cellar Selves so they work for you, not against you. The fire of stage four eliminates habits or patterns that are rigid, both softening and strengthening you at the same time. You become bold and courageous, willing and able to adapt to change with greater agility.

Risk-Taking

One of the gifts of stage four is that it makes room for new impulses that would've seemed out of character before. This begins as innocent experimentation. Because your old life is over and your new life has yet to form, the empty space within you invites you to act.

Before your LifeQuake, the adolescent part of you may have showed up wherever you lacked discipline, refused to take responsibility, or didn't listen to those wiser than you. In this stage, a more mature "inner teenager" emerges, expressing the urge to individuate in a healthy way. Rather than rebel against an outer authority, you begin to listen to an inner authority, even if it prompts you to go beyond your comfort zone and take a risk. This inner authority will move you to ask yourself, "What inspires me now?"

Despite being un-athletic and prone to motion sickness, I was inspired to try hang-gliding during my stage four passage. Even "tossing my cookies" on my instructor midair didn't deter me. Risk-taking took another form for Boyd Willat, creator of *The Day Runner*, the appointment-book system that revolutionized time management. Prior to forming his company, Boyd had been quite the worldly adventurer and was no stranger to physical danger. Ironically, however, it wasn't until his business went global that he would learn about engaging his emotional self.

When his company expanded in anticipation of going public, he handed over its helm to new management. As a result, Boyd felt exiled from the organization he'd created. "I was so agitated that I couldn't restrain my emotions," he recalled. "For the first time in my life, I ranted and raved ... in front of people I never would have before. But ultimately, it was quite liberating."

For Suzy Prudden, author and pioneer of a new mind/body/spirit approach called *Metafitness*, stage four initially meant unbridled freedom. Giving up her television show, fitness studio, and the busy schedule of teaching all day was a double-edged sword. "I'd been like a caged bird, and it was as if the doors flew open and I started to fly," she recalled. "The problem was I didn't know which direction to follow, so I tried them all. I had a wonderful time, but I had no control." This feeling of "no control" is often followed by a wave of intense fear. As the novelty of newfound freedom wears off, uncertainty springs up. You're in uncharted waters, and crossing to the other side requires continuing to "not know and still go".

Send in the Clowns

It takes courage to laugh when the universe has you deep in the cosmic fryer, but humor can be your salvation at this time. I grew up in a very conservative Catholic suburban neighborhood; these weren't the mean streets of Brooklyn. One Sunday morning as my family of six all piled out of the house to go off to church, we were stopped dead in our tracks—the beige exterior of our '68 Buick had been doused with bright red paint. We all knew that this wasn't the work of vandals. My father, a compulsive gambler, had been to Las Vegas again and the loan sharks were putting him on notice that the next time he was late paying his gambling debts, the red stains wouldn't be paint! The look on the pastor's face as we pulled into the parish parking lot filled me with humiliation. I longed to have a normal family, and now everybody knew we weren't. Having healed the place in my body where I held the shame of that candy-apple paint job, I can now laugh along with everyone else when I tell the story in seminars and imitate Father McFadden's expression as we filed into church.

At this point, you may panic and feel the impulse to backpedal to the safety of the life you left behind. But the old values and faulty patterns no longer work. Suzy Prudden attempted to give workshops and major lectures again. "I was paid $5,000 for a one-night lecture," she said. "It was thrilling. But when no one showed up, I was devastated." Boyd Willat invented new product lines, none of which succeeded until stages five and six. Because the soul's energy is completely consumed with internal transformation at stage four, very little in the external world will take root.

Accessing your sense of humor contributes to your transfunctionality, which helps you adapt to crisis-driven circumstances. Humor releases resistance to change, thus increasing endorphins (the joy chemicals) in the brain that lead to enlightened problem solving. By using humor, you'll move through stage four and life in general, at a higher vibration level.

Humor realizes its fullest potential by expanding your perception of reality. By releasing the shame that kept your Cellar Selves in the darkness, you accelerate your ability to embrace all parts of you. Through this acceptance, you more fully identify with who you really are. Don't be surprised if you have spontaneous moments when you see life as one big cosmic joke, executed by a God that looks like Wanda Sykes (black female comedian who left a prestigious job on the comedy writing staff for Chris Rock to do stand up)!

Here's a helpful exercise: Write an autobiographical story from your childhood, but do it twice. Write the first version as if it were a soap opera, making it as melodramatic as possible. Write the second one through the eyes of a comedy writer. If you think about it, comics take painful scenarios and make them funny. Many comics had tragic childhoods. By traversing these seven stages, you're learning to reinterpret events so that they now provide the raw material for your evolution. Give yourself comic relief by using your imagination to change the story of your past. Only you can reinvent the trauma/drama of your childhood so that you can extract the gold that is hidden in your Cellar.

The Devil Made Me Do It

At this stage, your old persona is no longer a heavy curtain you can hide behind. As you explore your Cellar Selves, you may stumble into shadow aspects that appear evil, wicked, or dark. When you've denied and repressed parts of yourself, you may call in experiences that compel you to become more aware of them. For example, one client was stalked by a fugitive who was a serial rapist that had escaped his former country. This forced my client to come to terms with her own hidden rage toward men.

Some of those I interviewed believed that they'd been visited by real demons. Others interpreted their harrowing experiences as holographic images produced by their own minds. Those who had such occurrences shared one major personality trait: they had all overly identified with the spiritual, moral, or religious side of their nature. By denying their dark side, they relegated it to the shadows of their unconscious. Just the act of venturing into this part of your self may actually feel overwhelming.

While deep in stage four, I had one such encounter with a dark, ominous force. A friend had asked me to house sit while she was away. As I bid her farewell, I complimented her on a piece of jewelry she was wearing, something she referred to as her witch's amulet. *Witches,* I thought, startled. *Why would anyone admit to being a witch?*

While meditating in her home that night, I felt a cold, ominous energy enter the room. I looked up, and there in the corner of the ceiling was an image of my friend, cloaked in black. She beckoned me to help her. Though frightened, I searched for a rational explanation for what I was seeing. Again, my intuition took over. I called out to be surrounded by Divine Love. Suddenly, I left my body and was drawn upward into a column of golden light. The dark entity was then simultaneously drawn into it as well.

To this day, I'm not sure what really happened that night, but I do believe that what we're afraid of, we attract. Further, the vulnerability of this stage can crystallize our disowned selves into fear-based holographic images, just like when you were a kid and saw a scary monster in the closet. If you were lucky enough to see a therapist as a child, he or she might've helped you see that the scary monster represented your math teacher, who made you feel dumb for not mastering fractions, for example. But the good news is that by focusing on who you really are, your Wholy Self, all these fear-based parts of you can transform.

Prior to this incident, I was unaware of my fear of witches. If you have an experience with either a person or entity that scares you or that you judge, ask yourself, "What do I disown in myself that this person represents, or what triggered emotion is this person's behavior mirroring for me?"

The frightening experience in my friend's home proved to be a turning point in my understanding of the true nature of evil. When we disown a part of ourselves by judging it so severely that it is driven into the subconscious realm, stage four will draw that part of the denied self to the surface to be integrated. It also often provides a necessary clue to your calling in life.

I had left the psychoanalytical model behind when I sold my practice in stage three, and I was suspicious of people with no academic credentials who claimed to be healers. The friend for whom I'd house sat for was friendly with a number of people who called themselves white witches and used light to manifest healing. I feared the spiritual power that these light workers seemed able to access. This experience was a turning point and prelude to stage five, where I began working with energy masters who used the power of divine love to heal.

In stage five of my LifeQuake, facing my fear of claiming this kind of power allowed me to walk into a room of corporate Doubting Thomas-types and access the light to transform the negative energy in the conference hall. Had I not experienced the transformation of that dark energy that entered the room that night, I would've resorted back to my intellect and given a very heady talk—backed by research and a PowerPoint presentation on intuition as a leadership skill. I had learned not to be afraid of collective fear and judgment and instead instructed them in an exercise to expand their heart energy. After completing my presentation, their feedback indicated that the exercise had indeed shifted their perceptions, and to my surprise, I received a standing ovation.

Here's an exercise: Have a dialogue with a part of yourself that you are ashamed of. If you can't think of one, go back to a moment when you had a murderous thought about someone or judged a particular person with intense resentment. Any time you have an extreme reaction to another person, that person will represent a disowned part of yourself or a trigger of judgment. Write about your inner demons as if you were writing a script. Make your observer self be the questioner, but give the characters names. When you pose questions to them, listen to their response. Ask questions with genuine curiosity, such as, "Hey, Hitler, what are you really afraid of that makes you want to annihilate your boss?" Hitler: "He doesn't deserve to be a manager. He is a terrible leader. I could do a better job." As the observer, listen and write your response. Allow the voice of the angry tyrant to keep ranting until there is no more left to write.

When you were a child and were dependent on your parents, you learned to suppress these urges. Now, however, they may contain the energy you need to recognize your desire to be more powerful in your job or in a personal relationship.

In the Heat of the Night

The demons we face aren't always other people. If you chose alcohol, drugs, (legal or illegal), workaholism, or other distractions to deny stages one and two, you probably crashed and burned in stage three. For some, stage four begins by entering an inpatient treatment facility—here is where the real work begins. Withdrawal from whatever crutches you've used can feel like hell. Going it alone is rarely a good idea. If you can't check yourself into a treatment facility, I strongly urge you to seek individual therapy with a trained specialist in chemical dependency or addiction. At the very least, join one of the anonymous twelve-step programs that are all available online now, while taking a close look at anything you've been doing to excess that is now causing you to spiral downward.

Confronting addictions to long-held beliefs is sometimes even more difficult than addressing substance addictions. In stage four, withdrawal from addictions of any kind thrusts intense emotions to the surface. Stripped of your old identity, you may be flooded with a tidal wave of feelings that well up inside you. At this point, your number one priority is to release these feelings. This gives you the opportunity to more fully develop two of this stage's building elements: *courage* and *compassion*. It takes both to stop using buffers and Band-Aids, but the payoff is enormous, if you can feel vulnerable without abandoning yourself. Bringing compassion and courage to the raw, naked you is the core of learning intimacy.

Shifting the Body's Landscape

It's important to understand that you're going through an expansion of consciousness that is part of the overall forward movement of your evolution. A spiritual acceleration is taking place that affects you on every level. As your consciousness evolves, your body follows suit. Adjustments in your eating and exercise regimens will occur, sometimes effortlessly, sometimes erratically, as your needs change. Old patterns may resurface. Unusual cravings, binge eating, even anorexia are not uncommon. Rather than judge these changes, though, see them as signs that your body is undergoing wholesale change.

Suzy Prudden recalled, "I went through the whole range. When I first left fitness, I was anorexic but not in the usual way. I knew I was too thin, but it was as though my spirit had left my body. As I went further into the 'wilderness,' I started eating like there was no tomorrow. This scared me, so I began compensating by vomiting whatever I ate. I knew I was coming back to the world when I stopped throwing up. I'd learned that what my body needed now for grounding was more protein than I allowed myself in the old days. Now when I'm working or on the road, I sometimes need red meat."

For Laura, a self-described overachiever and professional speaker, her body's response to stage four was quite vivid. "I'd moved to Los Angeles and felt the need for a physical discipline, so I attended a weekend yoga retreat. A complete novice, with no yoga background, I proceeded to approach the classes like I had aerobics in the past. At this point, the concept of listening to my body was utterly foreign. After two days of pushing myself to perform advanced poses in twice daily, ninety-minute sessions, my body reacted. While I was resting on my bed, my breathing became erratic, and I saw myself falling through a deep hole. The drop seemed endless. A voice I recognized as my own kept repeating, *I'm dying. I'm dying.* Frightened, I asked the teacher what was happening; she had no answer. After that weekend, my energy level dropped to almost nil. I slept ten to fourteen hours a day. My daily activities consisted of crawling from room to room and recording my dreams in my journal."

As a Jungian-oriented therapist, I received great inspiration and context for this client's Dark Night from Jung's writings on the "fall through the abyss" in his work on the soul's journey. This phenomenon marks the ego's release from an old concept of reality, resulting in temporary dissociation. Your identity has separated from the world so completely that you now perceive it as the illusion. Mystical experiences of this kind are often triggered by shock, trauma, or intense physical disciplines that require lengthy periods of deep breathing. Certain types of yoga, such as Ashtanga, Bikram, and Kundalini yoga, may be too rigorous during stage four. Listen to your body, and when in doubt, stop. Consider a less arduous style of yoga during this stage, perhaps something like gentle Kripalu or Amrit yoga.

After the yoga retreat, Laura's menstrual periods ceased for nine months. Though her gynecologist suggested birth control pills to resume her menstrual cycle, she intuited this wasn't the cure for her. At the end of the ninth month, she met a chiropractor at a friend's home. "He offered to treat me with a noninvasive, energetic healing approach known as the BEST technique. Though I accepted his offer with some skepticism, my period returned the next day. He explained to me that because the chakras coordinate to the endocrine system, my hormones had shut down to accommodate the acceleration. "Listening to my body instead of my gynecologist may have seemed risky, but by trusting my intuition that these physical changes had occurred after my yoga experience, I created space for an appropriate solution to arrive in its proper time," she recalled.

In stage four, what you eat and how you eat it is critical to supporting your body. While in my Cosmic Barbecue, I decided to give up eating animal protein. I constantly felt hungry and craved sugar, no matter how much soy and beans I ate. Unfortunately, in becoming a vegetarian, I hadn't realized that my body required a denser type of protein. My cravings were an indication of low blood sugar. Ironically, a vegetarian physician I consulted did a specific test that indicated I needed lamb. Though nauseated by the thought, I sat down to a plate of lamb chops and, to my surprise, devoured the meal. Your body doesn't lie—cravings reflect an imbalance.

If possible, consult a nutritionist or doctor during this time, one that utilizes a food regimen that's designed to your specific needs. To choose the appropriate practitioner, ask pointed questions in your initial phone inquiry.

To connect more deeply to your body's needs, begin each day by turning within. Use your breath to call in radiant light through the top of your head. Breathe this radiant light into your heart. As you place your hands over your heart, they will get warmer. Once you feel connected to your body, invoke an angelic presence, your higher self, or a spirit guide into the center of your heart. Ask the guide the following three questions, which can be answered directly or symbolically:

1. What do I need to know today? (Listen for a message or a symbol.)

2. What do I need to eat today? (Listen for a message or a symbol.)

3. What kind of exercise do I need today? (Listen for a message or a symbol.)

If you get a symbol, such as a picture of something, and you don't know how to interpret it, write it down and set the intention that the answer will come at just the right moment.

Though your body carries intuitive wisdom, hearing the answers may take some practice. The more you exercise your intuition, the stronger it becomes. By starting your day with this practice, eventually you'll enable yourself to hear the answers to these questions. Listening anew every day keeps your mind agile and avoids rote patterns and routines. In doing this exercise, you may hear your body tell you it wants jogging today, walking tomorrow, and yoga the next day. Next week, it could be completely different.

By stepping out of habitual thinking patterns, your mind becomes more agile, and your body becomes more flexible. Keep checking in, listening, and finding the courage to follow your body's message. This allows for a more organic reconstruction of your new life's design in stage five.

God, the Runaway Parent

Stage four can often involve a crisis of faith that forces you to relinquish your reliance on external sources for safety and security. A new, more authentic faith begins to emerge as you learn to trust your soul's unique path, even when it doesn't look like there is one. Having to proceed without any tangible proof is the challenge of the Cosmic Barbecue. This is where you learn the third building element—trust.

When ultimate despair fills your life, thoughts of suicide may arise. Suzy Prudden speaks of this difficult transition, having been through it herself: "People want to give up because the pain is too great, and their vision is too small. Mostly, they don't believe they have the right to have a vision of themselves as someone greater than [the person] they think they've been."

The lesson in stage four is to trust in a vision of yourself that you can't yet see or even feel because it hasn't take form. As you release an attachment to your old self-image, your authentic self will begin to emerge, your body wisdom will become your guide, even in the depths of despair.

Taking time every day to sit with your fears, locating where they are in your body, and breathing through them at their most intense will loosen their hold on you. Further, once you have met the emotions you may have disowned in your prior life, invoke and receive the radiant light from universal consciousness, what some may call divine love right into the pain or discomfort. This creates alchemy – lead into gold. Strangely enough, embracing the thing you think will break you is often times liberating beyond your wildest expectations.

Excavating the Diamonds

Directly embracing parts of the Cellar Self that sabotage you is important, but there are also highly evolved parts of the Cellar Self that must be embraced with equal attention.

Jim, a corporate lawyer, came to see me after going through a traumatic divorce. The collapse of his marriage thrust him into stage four. The depth of his pain made him extremely vulnerable. This opened him to experience a part of himself that he'd repressed since the age of eight, his psychic abilities. His fundamentalist upbringing instilled in him a deep fear of these abilities. "Sometimes I can literally read people's minds and feelings, and it terrifies me," he confessed. I explained that the trauma of his divorce had laid him open, leaving him in a state of hyper-vulnerability, allowing his psychic abilities to resurface. As he surrendered to the pain and grief of his lost marriage, the telepathic episodes receded in intensity, and his intuition integrated with his analytical mind.

Not only did he find that he trusted his instincts in work-related matters more confidently after his divorce, but the experience of keeping his heart open throughout his life deepened his compassion for others as well. Sustaining a loving nature in the face of pain accelerates the development of this heart-centered spiritual muscle and quickens your adeptness to hearing the call of stage five.

If you used the tools in the previous chapter, the crisis of stage three may have either softened or blasted your heart open more deeply. While interacting with your Cellar Self in stage four, it's important to engage in rampant acts of self-compassion and forgiveness. It encourages you to see and embrace all parts of yourself. Think about it. If you judge the denied parts with vicious contempt, why would they ever come out and show themselves? Extend compassion to every part of you as you journey through the underworld of your consciousness. At the very least, being compassionate about your fears and limitations can provide the kind of real self-soothing that doesn't sedate your feelings.

Working at the Car Wash and Other Vocational Fears

For most people, the greatest practical fear in stage four is that they'll be forced to take a subservient job or end up homeless. Though it seems plausible, this is rarely the case. Keep in mind, though, what we fear, we attract. While in stage four, I had very little energy and was incapable of working with psychotherapy clients. To avoid emotionally taxing myself, I took a day job as a receptionist in a chiropractor's office and a night job as a hostess in a restaurant. My family, friends, and colleagues were mortified. Initially, I felt intense shame, but over time, I experienced gratitude for doing simple work in a healing environment. I still hadn't figured out what I was going to do next, but working these low-stress jobs allowed me to gather strength as I made my way through stage four.

Simplifying your life is critical during stage four. By doing so, you redefine what it means to take a risk. The risk here involves surrendering your dated image to the unformed identity crystallizing inside. Professionally speaking, if you're attached to a certain image of yourself, this transition can be difficult.

Boyd Willat's identity was rooted in his image as patriarch of his company. Accustomed to always being in control, everything changed after he hired a new CEO. Surrendering his role proved more difficult than he'd anticipated. "I was not as noble as I would have liked," he reflected. "I felt displaced."

Remember, this is an embryonic period. Within this empty space, a new you is taking form. Like being pregnant, your energy is being used for the inner work being done. So if you find yourself extremely fatigued, don't be alarmed. Try to accommodate the need as best you can. Whether that means a quick catnap or brief meditation at your desk, honor the impulse without judgment.

Shake, Rattle, and Roll

The last half of stage four overlaps with the onset of stage five. Because this model is unique in its expression with every person, encountering your disowned selves, getting clear about your soul purpose, and designing your new life's blueprint may blend a bit. Vocationally, as you begin to engage new work interests, be careful not to take on too much too soon. If you've not finished the healing work that becoming a transfunctional self requires, you'll be thrown back into stage four.

Believing I'd completed my healing and was ready to be a professional again, I gave a corporate seminar at ARCO. I thought my talk at ARCO would be my coming-out party; instead, it was my swan song for about eighteen months. Because I hadn't done any public speaking for two years, on the day before the seminar I engaged a healer friend for an energy treatment that would ground me, so that I could project confidence and power. At the end of the session, I suddenly experienced electrical charges shooting through my body, accompanied by a drilling sound in my head. After my body calmed, I went home. That night as I got into bed, the drilling sound continued. I began having visions of a beehive, complete with a queen bee and worker bees.

I thought I was going crazy. A voice inside said, "The queen is symbolic of the Wholy Self, what some call the oneness consciousness or God. The worker bees are your sub-personalities in service to the queen." This was my introduction to the concept of the Wholy Self. As I waited to go on stage for my talk, the ground beneath me trembled. When I asked a friend if we were having an earthquake, she said no. It was at this point that I realized the quaking was coming from inside me.

The next day when I told my spiritual mentor about my vision, she said matter of factly, "Oh, the bee story. That is a classic spiritual initiation vision." When I mentioned my body shaking, she suggested to me that the next time it happened, I should eat something with real sugar in it. I did so, and the shaking stopped immediately. When I asked her to explain what had happened, she told me about the Kundalini, an energy phenomenon best understood and articulated by practitioners of yoga. The Kundalini is part of the bridge from the electrical system in the physical body to the invisible chakras in the etheric body. Its energy serves as an evolutionary mechanism in the body. It's triggered when the individual is ready for an acceleration of his or her electromagnetic energy.

I continued to shake, rattle, and roll every day for hours at a time. The power surges came in full force, consuming my life for a considerable period.

Many people, however, have Kundalini openings that don't incapacitate them. While counseling a young film director, he recounted having been awakened from a dream with the same experience of loud humming in his head and shots of electricity coursing through the top of his head. Thankfully, it lasted for only a minute; subsequently, the feeling manifested as increased intuition, along with a temporary craving for vast amounts of protein. I encouraged him to follow his body's instinct, as it may have needed to be more grounded while the Kundalini energy integrated his visible physical body with his invisible etheric body.

As we are receiving information from the health sector on the effects of 5G and its radiation effects, it is never more important than now to be practicing meditation, yoga nidra, and any other techniques for stimulating alpha and theta brain waves. This will strengthen the immune system and upgrade your etheric body for your kundalini to function and support optimum health.

The Agony and the Ecstasy

Stage four is designed to help you integrate your higher consciousness and subconscious states of awareness. People who come into your life at this time are critical teachers. For most of my life, I denied the existence of the irresponsible, selfish-teenager part of me, choosing instead to see myself as a self-sacrificing healer. Not surprisingly, during this time I met many people who were unapologetically self-focused. Clearly, I needed to look at what I had judged as negative in others and make peace with the character inside myself that they personified. You can do the same. For example, if someone moves you to anger that you can't explain, find the rage they're triggering in your body before confronting them. Then ask yourself, "What is this person mirroring that I don't outwardly express?"

For Diane Miller, her harshest reflection came in the form of her fifth husband, who literally came to embody her inner terrorist. A reputable physician in the community, he had a violent temper. Diane's Cosmic Barbecue began while hiding, after he'd threatened to kill her. In the depths of her confusion and despair, she had a revelation: her abusive husband was showing her something she'd been denying. "I was vicious toward myself. I felt I'd been rejected by my father and went on this quest to find the guy who would finally love the 'me' that I couldn't love. I brought in a killer because I was murdering my own soul, bit by bit," Diane recalled. She vowed that if she survived this, she would hold no bitterness toward him. In beginning her new life, she created a ritual in which she adopted the wounded little girl that lived within her. Diane's story exemplifies how to bring compassion to the Cellar Selves as they emerge.

Relationships that reflect your evolving self also begin to appear. Suzy Prudden recalled, "As the old patterns about men fell away, I met people who had a spiritual base. I asked for quality people to come into my life and bingo—it happened! We do have a choice. When we step onto a path of this nature, the right doors open."

While going through stage four and all subsequent stages, it's critical to surround yourself with people who are dedicated to a path of evolution. One of the most painful losses you may go through is saying good-bye to relationships with people who spiritually slow you down. Jack Canfield of *Chicken Soup for the Soul* fame and author of many books on success speaks fervently about being around people who are committed to your dreams and the advancement of your consciousness. Having people around you who have faith in you when you have lost faith in yourself is critical to moving smoothly into the later stages of your LifeQuake.

For Larry, a self-described recovering co-dependent personality, stage four involved a decision to walk away from a twenty-year career as a struggling actor. His dream now was to become a successful writer. In his personal life, he realized he hadn't surrounded himself with people who encouraged his dreams. Growing up as the middle child in his family, he felt unseen, something that he had projected into his adult life. He rarely got any parts where he was on camera for very long, and the friends he hung out with made him feel like a "beautiful loser." A turning point came when he joined his buddies for a night of playing backgammon and poker. His friend Ric, an out-of-work actor who made his living gambling, tended to be Larry's biggest critic. When Larry beat Ric repeatedly at backgammon, Ric became vicious. Larry became overwhelmed with guilt because he saw his winnings as taking from his friend's livelihood. Later that night, Larry joined the poker game, where he lost all the money he'd won playing backgammon, and then some. Together, we explored his fear of "taking from others" and always giving more than he received. He came to understand that he was projecting an identity that was safe and had chosen friends who contributed to this image. A battle for his soul waged within him, as his ego struggled to stay identified with the old self.

Larry's recovery process involved dialoging between the rescuer part of him that was in charge and the disowned, needy-child Cellar Self (see the Toolbox section for exercise). I instructed him to give them a name. As I spoke to each of these parts in him, he experienced the vulnerability that asking for help triggered. We also explored what he received from the 'beautiful loser' label he wore so readily. Larry discovered that the title of beautiful loser kept him from facing his fear that success would bring more responsibility than he thought he could handle. I suggested he take on this fear with incremental changes.

He began taking his destiny into his own hands with a writers group of select people who were committed to contributing to each other's dreams. There, he could give his "helper part" healthy expression, while receiving help as well. Within this group, he gave himself permission to receive feedback on his writing. In reaching out to those who saw him as a winner, he began to work as a freelance writer in stage five of his LifeQuake.

It's extremely important that you surround yourself with people who empower you at this crucial juncture. Their support can carry you through your Dark Night, sustaining you when you're unable to do so for yourself. Group coaching online can also be a cost effective way to be supported and guided.

How Not to Barbecue Your Partner During His or Her Dark Night

Your chances of successfully negotiating your LifeQuake increase dramatically in the presence of an informed partner. Give him or her this book (or buy your partner his or her own copy). When Martin Rutte, co-author of *Chicken Soup for the Soul at Work* and his own book, *Project Heaven on Earth*, went through his LifeQuake, his wife took over as primary breadwinner during his "temporary retirement." A professional speaker and management consultant, Martin was in burn-out. For six months, he sat on the sofa and watched TV. For Martin's wife, Canadian actress Maida Rogerson, it was important to continue to live her own life. "Ongoing communication between the couple is important. But even more than that, remember that your spouse's frustration is not about you," Rogerson said. "Don't take their frustration personally. They're going through a major change and may project some of their fears onto you. Stay busy with outside pursuits and maintain dialogue. Keep enough closeness to provide the support they need without hurting yourself in the process."

For couples, this stage of the LifeQuake involves releasing old ideas about marriage and creating a more flexible way of being together that's suited to this new cycle.

Answering the Call

Once again, claiming the parts of you that were relegated to the cellar of your consciousness clears the way for receiving messages to your calling. In deciding what choices to make, it's important to distinguish a calling from a career. Unfortunately, your calling rarely reveals itself in a meeting with a vocational counselor. They often employ a linear approach to what your career strengths and talents are. A calling speaks to something deeper and is more expansive than simply the work you do. Opening to your calling requires an emptying of who you were before, in order to be open to that who you are now.

It also means to be available to listen to that which is calling out to you. So … what is it that is speaking? And how do you best listen for its message? The Wholy Self speaks to you all the time. It's here to help you align with your highest destiny. When you practice stillness every day, you make its information "avail-able" to you. This sets your personal evolution in motion, while quickening the end of your Cosmic Barbecue.

The Oxford English Dictionary offers one definition of the word "avail" as "to be of use". It comes from the Latin word *valeo*—to be strong. Being fully present on a daily basis creates great strength, which ultimately leads to your being of great spiritual use, no matter what it is you are doing. Given that we are all connected, when you open to your unique fullest potential, you move the entire universe forward with you as well.

Here is an exercise to help you hear your calling. Every day in your quiet time, set the following intention: "I'm ready to be directed to my calling". Ask the question, "How can I best serve? What is my next step? What can I do throughout the day to magnetize this calling?" Then listen. Setting aside this sacred time doesn't necessarily mean you'll get an immediate answer.

What it means is that you will be more present as you go about your day. This is part of listening. You've set an intention for very specific divine coincidences to show you how to do everything. For example, engage in three activities that inspire joy for you. Now, engage in a task you need to do that you don't find to be much fun while accessing the feeling of joy you had in the previous activities. For instance, many years ago, Dr. Barbara DeAngelis once told me that when she writes a book, she spends the morning playing, using that energy to infuse her writing. If you're completely present, you can hear your calling while doing the dishes.

A calling inspires you to understand the intrinsic value of even the most mundane task. There is no distinction in importance between organizing your desk and writing the great American novel. Therefore, the way you do everything requires the same dedication and reverence. It is an intrinsic part of your calling and is to be distinguished from what you do for a living.

By its nature, a calling may deepen the gap between the life you're creating and the one you left behind. The paradox here is that this distance can allow for objectivity, so you can see, in retrospect, the themes from your past that led up to this moment. These are further clues to your life lessons and, therefore, to your authentic purpose.

As I've mentioned, the stages of *The LifeQuake Repurposing Road-map* overlap and aren't always linear. This is never more apparent than when you're leaving stage four. Take heart. The fever of stage four has broken, and once you've embraced the rejected parts of your Cellar Self, you're well on your way to utilizing them as part of your calling. In stage five, you'll put into practice the messages you received in stage four. This opens the door to finding your mission in life, your vocation of destiny, and the new design for your entire life.

For Suzy Prudden, this meant embracing her food addictions and body issues. This moved her to an entirely new philosophy, one that teaches people to love their bodies just as they are. For more information on Suzy's work go to **suzyprudden.com** In the ensuing years since LifeQuake was first published, Suzy has gone on to include another company in her work which is to help authors become published using a smaller platform. Go to **ittybittypublishing.com** for more information.

For Boyd Willat, the message was to learn from his experiences in managing his former company, Day Runner. Consequently, he founded a system for organizations that allowed the employees to function at an even higher level of efficiency through improved communication. This company became *Sensa*, a pioneer in the field of ergonomically designed pens. Although Boyd went on to create other products (*Govino*, the plastic wine glass you can put in the dishwasher), the emotions he confronted in his Cosmic Barbecue led to his becoming passionate about exploring this domain without fear, engaging life without diversion into addictions. This discovery became part of his management style and how he coaches others who are dealing with the stressors of running a business.

Answering my call involved traveling to a foreign country under the most unlikely circumstances. I was sitting on the beach in Southern California, minding my own business, when a voice deep inside said, "You will discover your home in Peru… Machu Picchu." It seemed ridiculous. I was being advised by a voice in my head to go by myself to a country on the brink of civil war, while I still was recovering from a devastating illness. And, mind you, back then my idea of "roughing it" was a two-star hotel in Maui! But by this time, I'd learned that resisting these messages only resulted in further delay. So after repeated check-ins with my inner guidance, three days later I bought a round-trip ticket to Lima.

I had initially prearranged all my travel within the country. When I arrived though, I felt compelled to cancel all of my travel arrangements and just allow myself to be guided, moment-to-moment. Frightened, I began the journey that would change my life. Because this was one of the key sites for the Harmonic Convergence, it was nearly impossible for a *turista* to get into hotels without the help of a tour guide. Yet everywhere I went, the accommodations materialized.

I began to trust that I was truly being taken care of—that is, until I arrived at Machu Picchu, the spiritual mecca of which I had been foretold. Every hotel was booked. It was winter in Peru—and I was forced to sleep outside in the freezing cold. As morning broke, I was alone and shivering. Walking toward the train station, I questioned the message that had brought me here. I decided to head for the nearest travel office and go home. Within a short time though, an old woman dressed in black appeared on the road, out of nowhere.

She approached me and introduced herself. Her name was Madrina, Spanish for "godmother." She practiced a form of healing called shamanism; she worked miracles with the Peruvian Indians who were suffering from alcoholism. She invited me to tea. What I thought was going to be a lovely chat with someone who reminded me of my grandmother became a three-day adventure that turned my worldview upside-down. She shared her perspective on mental illness and its root causes.

This wise old medicine woman explained that my illnesses, visionary experiences, and other traumas created an opening in my consciousness that separated me from what most people experience as reality. It allowed me to move through a passageway to alternate parallel universes. I knew about parallel universes from quantum physics, so I was relieved to hear that this crack in my reality was not a symptom of cracking up. She also told me that I had the markings of a shaman, the kind of teacher who enters this path through a healing crisis.

I reasoned that if someone with a traditional background like mine had been put through a shamanic initiation, it must've been because I was destined to assist the mainstream culture. I realized my calling was to be a bridge for people transitioning from their obsolete tribal programming to a new reality, one meant to express their highest potential. I didn't know how I was to do it yet, but I was resolved to find a way to lend context to these mystical experiences so that others wouldn't feel as if they were losing their minds like I had.

That way was eventually provided after my return. One day, while in deep meditation, I was given the seven stages to *The LifeQuake Repurposing Roadmap*. Using them myself at first, it became my mission to give people a way to build adaptable, internal structures in their psyches that are unique to their own destiny. I also returned to teaching those people who worked in crisis driven corporate America how to anticipate the need for change and eliminate catastrophes as primary catalysts. As I often stress to executives who are in burnout and to anyone who wants the "secret" to discovering their soul purpose: find time to be still!

Having time in a place you can be totally silent can provide the environment for the Wholy Self to speak. Toward the end of Martin Rutte's six-month sabbatical, this Canadian Jewish man found his calling while on retreat at an Augustinian monastery. In contemplating his work as a management consultant, he realized that what was missing for him in his work was God. He was being called to bring spirituality into the workplace.

Clearly, traveling to foreign countries, spending time in a sacred environment like a monastery, and/or traveling into higher states of awareness through meditation all can open the door to reflection and the "Aha!" moment. Meditation and traveling, however, aren't the only ways to discover your mission or new vocation. Take a closer look at your past. Is there a theme that connects the interests that inspired you? For instance, as a child I loved Greek mythology. Coincidently, while in graduate school, my first therapist was a Jungian analyst. Carl Jung believed that mythology held important keys to the integration of the human psyche. In returning to my Jungian studies during my cosmic barbecue, I connected another dot: I had no idea that Jung, a Victorian era analyst, was an avid devotee of astrology. Inexplicably, I found myself drawn to books on this subject. So my childhood interest in Greek mythology, my early training as a Jungian therapist, and my passion for astrology converged. When I returned to private practice, I also incorporated astrology as a diagnostic tool that was particularly useful in uncovering one's soul purpose and calling. A person's astrology chart is a soul blueprint that can often show me where the blockages are in the body. That evolved into then incorporating my shamanic training to clear what is holding the client back, and then using astrology to advise the best timing for taking the next step.

Look at where the dots in your life connect. Examine where your past and present intersect for clues to your future destiny. Make a list of everything you've ever done that you enjoyed. Is there a repeated theme? Put the list under your pillow at night and allow your unconscious mind to connect the things you've loved to some future calling in a non-linear mode. You may be given a dream that directs you, or perhaps the form may come in surprising ways through divine coincidences.

Divine Coincidences

Hopefully, you've been taking note of divine coincidences throughout each of the preceding stages. But now that you've met your Cellar Selves, the divine coincidences that show up here directly engage your life's calling. People appear who pose insights into your calling. Ask yourself whether they genuinely support the new life you're leading. Every opportunity that appears is also a test to sharpen your skills of discernment.

A great technique for consciously creating synchronicity in tangible forms is to ask for a particular item to show up as an omen to indicate that you're on the right path. One client, a radio talk-show host, consulted me while in stage four. She was still recovering from her stage three crisis, ovarian cancer. Having worked intensively on the issues in her cellar that she believed caused the cancer, she now wanted to meet her soul mate. After discussing a symbol, she settled on lavender roses as her telling omen. She would know the man was right for her if he brought them on their first date. That man showed up within days with a single sterling rose, a rare variety of lavender. He ultimately became a healing force in her recovery, and later, the producer who took her radio show to a national audience.

The void of stage four poses another hidden advantage: by feeling removed from your former life and its routines, you're also able to see divine coincidences more readily. Synchronicity occurs because your raw, separate, vulnerable self is tuning in to your environment with heightened sensitivity and awareness. You now may notice which interests bring vitality with greater ease and mastery.

Acts of Courage

Once you've glimpsed your new path, your commitment to it will be tested. When Martin Rutte decided to bring the G-word (God) into the business world, his idea wasn't immediately met with open arms. Not surprising, his six-month sabbatical provided an internal strengthening of resolve. He knew there was nothing that held more passion for him than this calling. Eventually, the doors did open, although slowly at first. But as we will see in chapter seven when we revisit Martin's LifeQuake journey, it became an even bigger calling than he had imagined.

Sometimes, our calling comes to us accidentally or with a little push from the universe to embolden our courage. I hadn't spoken publicly in over two years when I agreed to give a talk to the Rotary Club. I wore a conservative suit and gave a safe talk on adapting to crisis driven change.

The president of the club was also the vice president of a major bank, who happened to love astrology. Somehow, he got wind of the fact that I also was an astrologer. The following week, when the Rotary Club's scheduled speaker fell ill, he asked me to return and speak on how planets in our galaxy were impacting the political climate. I feared that tomatoes would be thrown at the stage and that I'd be seen as some far-out, flakey psychic. It was one thing to apply the principles of astrology in the safety of my office and quite another to speak in front of an audience of conservative, mostly middle-aged men.

I ultimately accepted his invitation to return and give another talk. To my shock, it was well received. This opened the door and expanded my calling as a professional speaker to include pragmatic information about how the electromagnetic fields of planets in our solar system affect world events. It took a lot of courage, but as I became available to my calling, I realized that astrology could be another way to help people prepare for change and understand the meaning of the crises they were in. Further, now there are scientists like Bruce Lipton who perceive the vibrational impact that planets in our galaxy have on our earthly lives.

As you reach the end of stage four, opportunities that are part of your calling may come in ways that surprise you. They may do so because they don't fit with an image you have of yourself. I worked with a realtor who had a passion for matchmaking more than selling houses, but she couldn't imagine making money from becoming a marriage broker. Perhaps you're a corporate executive, and you find yourself drawn to massage or bodywork. The key is that when you think about actually doing that particular thing, is there more "aliveness" in your body? If so, as you begin to enter stage five, see your life now as an experiment. The trial-and-error period has begun.

Building Elements

Remember, the building elements of stage four are *courage, compassion, and trust*. It takes courage to walk away from what is inauthentic. It takes courage to experiment with taking risks. And it takes courage to face the valuable and scary parts of you that are submerged in the cellar. As your cosmic barbecue burns away your faulty identity, your heart opens to self-compassion, as well as greater compassion for the flawed humanity of others. This eventually leads you to trust the messages that come in great stillness and at the darkest moments. Moreover, it is the listening and the following of these messages that will lead you to your calling.

The Toolbox

The following exercise will help you embrace the parts of yourself that you consider both sacred and profane in the Cellar Self.

Name That Fear

Make a list of five things you are currently afraid of. After choosing one that you want to work with, find its location in your body. Breathe deeply into the place where it lives, exploring it as you do. What is its size and shape? Does it feel hot or cold? Stay with it; let it speak or appear to you as a living character or symbol.

What do you need to learn from this fear? Notice the emotional intensity around the fear. Now breathe even more deeply into it; think back to the very first memory you have of it. How old were you the first time you felt this fear? If you were a child, see yourself as that child, only this time ask a spiritual guide to be with you. You may feel more comfortable with someone you're familiar with, such as Jesus or Buddha or an angelic figure. Just allow the presence to show itself either visually or as merely a feeling of love. Your spiritual guide will now help you reinterpret this childhood event from a higher perspective. Allow the guide to show you why you chose to have this experience. By explaining its purpose in the context of your life lessons, you achieve a new understanding that transforms the fear. This allows you to release any residual blame in the process. Now see the guide merge with the child you. Allow the child to fill with light. Allow that light to fill your body here in the present.

Now revisit your list of current fears (e.g., your fear of leaving your job and ending up homeless). How are you currently experiencing the one you worked with? If fear is still present, make it even bigger and more intense. Breathe all the way into it, filling it with radiant light. Set the intention that you've installed a new pattern for addressing any subsequent fear. When the fear has subsided, ask the Wholy Self to give you a new symbol to show what your next step should be. Remember, that's all you need to know—your next step.

After you open your eyes, list any solutions/messages you received directly next to the coordinate fear. Do this exercise any time you're overwhelmed or anxious and can't access your inner guidance. Sometimes these fears will come up spontaneously, often in the middle of the night or early morning. Go through the exercise again. When fear presents itself, you have a great opportunity to move more easily into the subconscious realms. It opens a portal where you can directly confront your proverbial demons, transforming them once and for all.

Developmental Steps to Change Mastery

- ✓ You've embraced the denied parts of you kept in the Cellar.

- ✓ You've answered the call through your intention to avail yourself to a higher purpose, even if you aren't totally clear about the specifics.

- ✓ You've taken courageous risks that plant the seeds for your new life.

5

Designing the New Blueprint:
You as Architect and Apprentice

I have missed more than nine thousand shots in my career. I have lost almost three hundred games. On twen-
ty-six occasions, I have been entrusted to take the game
winning shot—and I missed. And I have failed over and
over and over again in my life. And that is precisely why
I succeed.

~ Michael Jordan

Onset

Stage five's onset occurs after the dust has settled just long enough
for a whiff of the future to reach your nostrils. It's like that moment at
the end of winter when your body says, "Whew! It's almost over!" And
you find yourself going to the closet for something bright and colorful
to wear. Only this isn't a spring fling you're getting dressed for—it's your
new life.

If you are reading this while still in any of the previous stages, know
this: opportunities will begin to crystallize at this stage. To fully actuate this stage, you've reclaimed the denied parts of you, emerged from
the cellar, and discovered that you're being called to a larger vision and
purpose. Notice that I didn't say that you've landed a dream job or discovered the path to your ideal career. Though we tend to think of higher
purpose in these terms, what you do for a living is just one aspect of
your soul purpose. Stage five is all about having the agility and faith to
continually retool your life, according to what is authentic in the moment.

The Holy Grail

The myth that most profoundly illustrates and empowers this stage of your LifeQuake is the twelfth-century legend of the Holy Grail. One of the aspects of myths that make these timeless stories so powerful is that we see the hero handling all kinds of unexpected challenges and mishaps. It doesn't matter one bit how bizarre or devastating the twists and turns are in the road; in fact, all of that is the stuff of true adventure. Your life is likewise a remarkable journey. And seeing it as an adventure that has intrinsic significance will help you see that mistakes and wrong turns aren't failures—they're both the hammer and the chisel that craft and refine your very being.

The grail myth has many interpretations. Though its primary symbol is the chalice, it's also been depicted as a bowl—and in *The Da Vinci Code*, even as a woman. All of the grail symbols, however, have one thing in common: they represent the divine feminine function in the human psyche.

In stage five, it represents the part of every man or woman that is an open cup, going beyond the limited information of one's experience to a level of receptivity for downloading, using, and then releasing information from the universe. Like a gold chalice, the key to having a life that supports us is making sure the container itself is durable and receptive to new information moment to moment. Learning to connect with the Wholy Self fills any cracks where fear of change still resides. In all grail stories, the hero is put through a purification process (such as one you may have experienced in the cosmic barbecue of stage four) to prepare for the attainment of the grail.

My favorite version of the grail story actually comes from a movie, a very silly one called *Monty Python and the Holy Grail*. Part of what must be embraced in stage five is the willingness to be silly and outrageous and think outside the box. Like many grail stories, this one is set in the time of King Arthur. Its irreverent take on the search for the Holy Grail is a humorous illustration of the passage we go through in stage five.

In the Python version, King Arthur ventures off to gather great knights from various kingdoms and bring them back to sit at the Round Table in Camelot, but even when he finally gathers his knights, he has to change direction. Upon returning to Camelot, Arthur realizes his quest has been a decadent distraction and decides to abandon it, bewildered about what to do next. Then he and the knights receive a vision: God demands that he act, not as His supplicants but as equals. He commands them to go on a quest for the Holy Grail. But Arthur and his knights do not have horses so they climb on pretend ponies while their servants bang coconuts together to simulate the sound of hooves. Not only must they be inventive with their mode of transportation, but each of the actors who play Arthur or his knights has multiple characters he must play in the film as well.

Arthur convinces the knights to follow him on an adventure, despite their desire to not leave Camelot. Treacherous events ensue, including a comedic version of the Black Plague and a rescue operation at the Castle of Anthrax, where seductive illusions and beautiful women lead the knights astray. In the end, when Arthur finally arrives at the Castle of Arrggh where the Grail chalice is kept, he discovers that he'd already been to this castle but was unable to get past the French guards. With one lone knight remaining at his side, Arthur slays the demented Black Knight and the killer rabbit, climbs the castle steps, and enchants the French guards.

Many aspects of stage five are like this story. You may be short on resources as you begin this stage. Like King Arthur, who used coconuts to simulate horsepower, you will need to use your imagination to progress on your path and assume different identities as you experiment with your new life. Then you may arrive at what you imagined would be an ideal destination, only to find you aren't where you'd hoped to be. Sometimes, that's a good thing, and the destination is better than what you'd imagined; sometimes, where you end up isn't aligned with your purpose. Like King Arthur, you'll need to listen for God's subtle voice at such moments. This God isn't the overlord holding you accountable for your wrongs, but a partner and guide whose greatest joy is seeing you possess your very own Grail, and with it, the understanding that what matters most is the journey itself, not the destination. In your Life-Quake journey, though, the key to owning your Grail is the mastery of adaptation.

Just as each of the main actors in the film plays many roles, so must you wear various vocational hats in stage five. You're called on to be both the apprentice *and* the master architect. The job of the apprentice is to learn and learn and then learn some more, while the master architect from your heart to your brain designs the blueprint. Like the journey that King Arthur takes to numerous castles in search of the Grail, only to find it at the beginning, you design a blueprint for your new foundation that returns you to your essential self. Trial and error is part of the territory at this stage. You must reinterpret failure altogether; conventional wisdom simply has no place in stage five.

So, part of recovering from stage 3 and 4 in this stage requires engaging a practice that can calm the heart so you can engage this stage as the adventure it can be. A resource for creating masterful heart/brain coherence comes from The Heart Math Institute. "Self-induced positive emotions increase the coherence in bodily processes, which is reflected in the pattern of the heart's rhythm. This shift in the heart rhythm in turn plays an important role in facilitating higher cognitive functions, facilitating emotional stability and calmness." **heartmath.org/resources**

A Flexible Foundation

In this stage, evolutionary mastery of change means the willingness to envision yourself as flexible, resilient, and authentic. You do this by taking the opportunities and inspirations that come to you and implementing them. Those that work become part of your new foundation, and those that don't go in the dumpster. Now is when you realize the wisdom in the old saying, "Nothing ventured, nothing gained."

Etch A Sketch-ing Your "Wholy" Holy Grail

Do you remember playing with an *Etch A Sketch* toy as a child? In 2019, Google Chrome Labs released a free, online, open source recreation called Web-A-Skeb, but in order to evoke your child self through the tactile quality of Etch a Sketch, I still suggest playing with the original, if you can. The square red frame had a glass window that functioned as a drawing board. You drew images by using the knobs on the frame and then turning it over and shaking the frame to make the picture disappear. If you didn't erase the picture after showing off your Picasso-like creation, you couldn't draw a new picture. So, of course you shook the frame and started over. No-brainer, right? But we don't do it like that in life. We try to draw over the old design (cut or build an addition to the life we have) rather than start fresh. Imagine how creative you could be if you approached designing your new life as though the world were a blank canvas or an adult version of an *Etch A Sketch*. You could attempt a new project, new relationship, new job, even a new form of exercise the way you did as a kid—with playful curiosity and spontaneity.

The point here is this: don't take yourself too seriously. Allow for creativity, while continuing to refine and correct your course. What you're really doing is clearing your psyche so that you can hear the truth if you need to change course.

Another toy that can keep you in the adventurous, creative spirit of childhood is the *Magna Doodle*, a magnetic drawing board that comes with a special pen. Writing with this pen forms a black line on the white screen. At the bottom of the *Magna Doodle* is a slider that erases the screen when it's moved back and forth.

During stage five, I often tell clients to buy a real *Magna Doodle* and write on it every day. At the top of the board, I tell them to write what they believe is their calling. I also have them write their vision of the coming day on it in a few short sentences—the way they want their day to be, as well as what they want to accomplish.

This can be your blueprint as well. Get a *Magna Doodle* and write an affirmation that inspires you to feel like a hero on an adventure. For example: "I dissolve the dragons of fear as I embrace change in all its manifestations." At the end of the day, review it. Don't judge what was not accomplished or how you did that day. Merely note it. Then erase the screen, and write a new script the following day. The script may be the same one from one day to the next, or it may be altered, as you discover what has vitality for you and what doesn't. The key is to practice beginning every day by either writing a new vision on your *Magna Doodle* or sketching a picture that symbolizes it on an *Etch A Sketch*. Both toys provide an opportunity to build an authentic life with a playful hand and an agile mind, one that keeps you adjusting the picture as you continue the adventure.

What It Appears to Be

As your energy returns, opportunities and challenges will present themselves. You'll explore or be presented with new career possibilities, lifestyle choices, and relationships, and, if you have the freedom to move about geographically, even new environments. Some of these choices will resemble your old picture of success, triggering dated, over-achiever patterns. You may be tempted to go into your new life at full throttle, using a template that worked before.

The key to making progress through stage five is in your ability to access the Wholy Self. If you've learned to check in with the Wholy Self in meditation every morning, stage five will feel like a grand experiment—one in which you possess an inspired willingness to keep drafting a new blueprint, over and over. If you choose to go it alone, frustration and confusion can mount as you "trial and error" your way through it. This gives rise to the question of whether or not you're on the right track. But that question gets answered quickly when you attempt to go back to the old way of living, only to find that boredom and lethargy throw you back into stages one or two.

Ultimately, there are no mistakes. If you find yourself back in a previous stage, simply apply some of the exercises in those previous stages and focus on their building elements. For example, if you've taken a job that, on the one hand, has returned a feeling of financial stability, yet you find yourself tired at the end of the day, practice *keen observation*. Notice what you enjoy doing in the course of your day. Where does your mind have the most interest? What tasks or activities do you have energy for?

You may not need to give up the job, just work at it differently. Now, more than ever before, the workplace has been transformed to allow you to work from anywhere. Try rearranging your day so that you alternate between tedious tasks and those you enjoy. Experiment with your workflow. Does rescheduling when you do things make a difference in your energy at the end of the day? If not, then it might be appropriate to reconsider the work or profession you've chosen, as it may not be supporting you by utilizing your best abilities and talents.

You might consider taking up a hobby that brings you joy, while remaining at the job that gives you a paycheck. One of my clients felt bored and stuck while working as a secretary, so she started bingeing on sugar when she came home at night. After working with the stage one exercises and observing what gave her energy, she discovered a passion for helping teenage girls improve their body image. She followed this interest with lighthearted curiosity over a period of years and eventually left secretarial work behind. She now works full time with young girls.

What Really Is Happening

Like all the other stages, how stage five appears outwardly and what's going on in your evolution may not match. Each stage is unique and has its own natural beginning and end. You'll know you've reached the end of stage five when you can be at peace, even when the ground beneath your feet isn't solid and firm. Pema Chodron has named this state "resting into groundlessness". She writes extensively about it in her book, *When Things Fall Apart*. The ability to rest into groundlessness is a substantial attainment; once you feel it, you'll have a sense of inner safety that doesn't rely on external supports. For many people, the challenge of a LifeQuake is exactly what the mind and emotions need in order to reach this state of inner certainty.

In stage four you may have experienced yourself as separating completely from the tribe and its belief system. You may have felt alone and alienated, consumed by two big questions: "Who am I?" and "Where do I fit in?" Now that you're back from this inner desert, you're rejoining your old community or branching out into new ones, and your challenge is to speak and live from your truth. "How do I engage in a way that is authentic and harmonious with who I know myself to be today?" This requires a very distinct form of bravery. It's not the heroic bravado of days gone by; it's a quiet courage that dares to tap into your essential core and speak from there.

Every time you access the Wholy Self and speak from this level of truth, you recognize this is who you want to be. You sacrifice old identities, habits, and structures. Instead of eating oatmeal every day, you listen to your body and see what it hungers for. You no longer relegate sex (with a partner or yourself) to a particular night as per old habits; you feel into when and where sexual intimacy emerges, as a desire bubbling up from your core. You may find yourself wanting to make love spontaneously in the middle of the day—or not at all for a period of time. What's important is to shift from rote, automatic behavior, and listen to what you truly want and need, and move from there.

The more you let go of what is superfluous and focus on your higher purpose, the better you'll feel. Separating the proverbial wheat from the chaff leaves you with what is truly essential to a vital life. Each experience is but one in a series of successive approximations to your authentic life. As the new blueprint is continually refined on a daily basis, you see how you've become the guinea pig in your own experiment. "A daily basis?" you might ask. Yes, this isn't a blueprint for a solid structure that is fixed and earthquake-resistant. This kind of retrofitting is all about wakefulness and staying present to the moment.

In stage five, you may have a vision of your authentic life, but it'll be tested like every grail adventure. See your life now as a great experiment; every day you're testing the vision and honing the implementation. Castles that appear to hold great promise may turn out to be illusions like the Castle of Anthrax in the Monty Python story. Even illusions have a purpose, however, as they often show us what isn't aligned with who we are now.

Mission and Purpose

So how do you determine whether you're on or off track? There are several ways to handle this dilemma. By the end of stage four, you've activated your higher purpose; now, in stage five, it's time to clarify and actuate your mission. Though these concepts have an overlap, there are some key distinctions. Your values and the qualities you want to express come from your soul's purpose. You know you are ready to write a mission statement when you have an initial sense of what you want to accomplish and contribute. I often encourage clients to write two mission statements: one for their vocation or business and one for their personal life. For example, my mission statement is as follows: "My mission is to globally assist awakening people into eliminating catastrophic crisis as the catalyst for change, through activating their joyous, soul purpose." My inner purpose is to experience my life as a continual lesson in refining my heart. A mission statement has three components: it's concise, it inspires you, and it has a target audience you want to reach.

For Luciano Copete, one of the LifeQuake pioneers we met in stage three, having a personal and professional purpose is essential. In his design business, his company's mission statement is: "We combine an idea with an artful design that best represents the functionality of the product, organization, or company." When asked about his inner purpose, he replied, "To know my brain, my soul, and my senses the best I can, so they serve as guidance for my instincts to follow the honest path for me."

As you approach building your life in this stage, it'll provide the cornerstone to your foundation. Even if you're not clear about the specifics of your ideal life yet, when opportunities or people come in to your life, deciding where to put your energy gets easier when your values, talents, and mission are clear. Ask yourself whether something is aligned with who you are now and what you want to contribute to the world. For example, if you aspire to be a writer, you know the talent you possess, but what impact do you want to have on your audience? Do you want to entertain? Do you want to bring cutting-edge information to the public?

Do you want to change people's psyches? What turns you on the most in other people's writing?

If you have a vicious inner critic who shoots down your ideas or vision on your *Magna Doodle* or *Etch A Sketch*, sit in a chair, and then move to a place in the room where you can act out the voice of the critic. Speak to the empty chair that represents your conscious self from the voice of the critic as you stand in that other place in the room. Let the critic really rip. Say out loud all the messages it has been running through your mind. Then, move back to the chair and become your conscious self with curiosity. Ask any questions of the critic you need to, such as: "What is your function inside of me? What are you afraid of? What do you need from me to feel safe?"

Get out of the chair and move back to the place in the room where the critic was standing and answer these questions. When you're done with this part of the exercise, while still in the critic's space, close your eyes. As you breathe in, imagine a golden ray of light coming into the top of your head. Set the intention of breathing this light into every cell of your body. Out loud, call in the spirit of your Wholy Self to merge with your critic. Then ask to be shown: *How will you have me serve through the Wholy Self? What is my next step?* Write down whatever you experience.

Another way of discovering if you're on track with following your higher purpose and mission comes through dream interpretation. If you can't afford to work with a therapist trained in Jungian-based archetypal psychology, I recommend two books that can assist with your dreams: *Active Dreaming: Journeying Beyond Self Limitation to a Life of Wild Freedom* by Robert Moss and *Dreamwork for the Soul* by Rosemary

Guiley. Moss' book is a way of being fully of this world while maintaining constant contact with another world, the world-behind-the-world, where the deeper logic and purpose of our lives are to be found. Guiley's book provides an understanding of lucid dreaming and how to use dreams to heal illnesses. Both are available in paperback. Although I use dream interpretation with all of my coaching clients, from time to time, I do offer online courses in how to use dreams to discover your calling.

The purpose of this practice is to call upon your subconscious mind during sleep to give you information, sometimes in symbolic form, about how to proceed with a decision you may be confused about. Let's say you were to be offered an opportunity to work in a field that requires leaving the country. This may bring up fear. If you have a family, and their wellbeing is part of your higher purpose, you have a lot to consider. The conscious mind may immediately reject this idea. The conversation in your head may go like this: "I can't take my kids away from their friends and community." Or "There's no way my ex will let me take them out of the country." However, when you sleep, you step out of the rational linear mind and can tap into the future in the dreamtime. I've received information about events that took place in my life six months after I dreamed them. One practice that can stimulate dream recall is to keep a blank book by your bed. Write tomorrow morning's date on a page. After the date, write three times: "As I awaken, I am remembering a dream that answers my question about ...". After writing it, affirm it out loud three times. "As I awaken, I am remembering the dream that answers my question about... .". Keep a glass or bottle of water by your bed. Take a sip of water after you do the verbal affirmations. When you awaken, take another sip of water. This may assist you in triggering your memory of your dream. Whatever you remember, even if it's just a feeling or an impression, write it in your blank book or journal.

Everyone can achieve dream recall, but it's like a muscle, the more you set an intention every night to remember your dreams in the morning, the more likely, over time, you'll remember them upon awakening. As you orient your mind toward problem solving from the right side of the brain, rather than the left, the unconscious mind becomes more conditioned to release information specific to your questions. Members of indigenous tribes share their dreams with each other every day. If you live with others, you can make this a practice to do at a joint meal. If you live alone, find a friend or colleague who might enjoy learning dream interpretation and share your dreams by phone or e-mail every day. The mere speaking of a dream can give you the "Aha!" moment you seek. As you're rebuilding your inner and outer life, taking the stress off the rational, conscious mind to make all your decisions is critical in this stage.

My clients have found dream interpretation to be a useful tool in keeping them aligned with their mission. Jane had been a corporate executive at a major movie studio for ten years, but her real dream was to produce independent films with positive messages. She left the studio, took a second mortgage on her house, and began to work as an agent for screenwriters, in the hope of acquiring scripts that she could sell through her relationships with motion picture production companies. Two years into the process, she had three deals in development with studios, but nothing moving forward into production. And practically speaking, she was running out of money.

Jane sought therapy with me to gain clarity as to whether she should give up her dream and get another corporate job at one of the film studios in Los Angeles. A friend offered to put in a good word for her with a marketing firm that serves the movie industry. Jane wanted to know if she should pass on any potential offer made to her. I encouraged her to go through the process of updating her résumé, meeting with the marketing director, and then noticing how she felt after the interview. I also encouraged her to pay attention to her sleeping dreams for guidance. The next day she woke up from a dream that indicated that she would be selling out if she went to work for the company she was interviewing with. I encouraged her to keep the appointment anyway.

Going through the steps of actually pursuing a job assisted her in remembering why she had gone into business for herself in the first place. She preferred setting her own schedule, working from home, and being her own boss. Observing her energy before, during, and after the job interview inspired her to bring new resolve and faith in her efforts as an independent producer. It also became clear that some of the screenwriters she was representing needed to go. She decided to release anyone whose script she'd not been able to get optioned by a production company in the past two years. The big quandary that remained was how to deal with her cash flow and the isolation she experienced from working at home.

She also discovered that she needed to create alliances with film companies who were producing projects that were naturally aligned with making a global difference. Her remedy came when she became acquainted with a production company that had made several socially significant films. She began working part-time out of their office as their mutual projects began to take off. Listening to her dream, rather than to her desperation and panic, allowed her to set a clear intention of what she wanted. Had she not experienced the full impact of job interviewing, however, Jane might not have had faith in her mission or in the message from her dream to be able to pass on the seductive lure of a steady paycheck.

Divine Coincidences

As in all the other stages, look for synchronistic cues from the outer world as another way of assessing whether you're on the right track. In the early stages of your LifeQuake, these cues are meant to guide you toward withdrawing from areas of your life that you've outgrown, so you don't have to bring in a catastrophe to get your attention. In stages four and five, the divine coincidences are meant to assist you in specifically understanding what your higher purpose and mission are. Moreover, in stage five, these synchronicities may function as en-"courage"-ment, with a big emphasis on the courage, so that you don't give up altogether on your commitment to live authentically. They also serve to redirect if you've gotten off course from your purpose. This is why you can't be consciously living the lessons of stage five until you've articulated and committed to a mission, as defined in your mission statement. The mission may change as you try things out, but it provides the foundation for your life.

To reiterate, as the first three stages of this process were about severing your obsolete identity with the outside world, stage four involves living in a void state, in which you may feel completely disconnected to everything around you. In stage five, you're reconnecting with the world but from a different place. You're learning to shed the programs you were raised with that demand societal conformity and are now relating to others from a more authentic truth. The key is practice and experimentation.

This isn't to say that in stage five you won't slip back into those programs. If living authentically brings with it pain or loss of other people's approval and support, you may try to re-embrace other people's values to feel safe again. However, the practice of working both with the inner world of dreams and the heightened awareness of your waking state will allow you to live more deeply in the moment. Through your powerful intention and awareness, this calls forth more seemingly coincidental events that bring meaning and direction through this uncharted territory. Therefore, pay close attention to the world around you now.

On and Off the Wagon

If embracing denied aspects of yourself in stage four involved confronting your addictions, then reconstructing your life in stage five may bring times when you fall off the proverbial wagon. This is because the blueprint you're constructing in this new cycle has to be revised or redirected.

Jacqueline worked with me to resolve the creative blockages that were interfering with her work as a sculptor. Along with her husband and child, she'd recently moved here from Europe, and although she liked America very much, she started turning to cocaine more frequently to inspire her art. She often spoke with great longing of her life before her marriage, when she'd supported herself as an artist in Italy for many years, even constructing her own house by the sea. She missed her adventurous life there. Jacqueline expressed deep frustration and disappointment that in her new life as a suburban mom, her drug usage had returned; previously it had been a habit she only engaged in at parties.

A painter for many years, after the birth of her daughter and transition to the States, she began sculpting. I observed that her life as a single woman mirrored her psyche. Her life was as liquid and fluid as the oils she used to paint. With no children or spouse, she could take off to Tibet at a moment's notice if she so desired. Now, she was working with a block of stone that weighed a thousand pounds, and the studio was an hour away.

Unconsciously, she'd changed the medium of her art and its location. This allowed her to follow the ocean as she traveled to the studio.

She also had created a project that would mean chiseling away, bit by bit, at everything that was not the man and child she saw within it. There was certainly nothing mobile about that, but it represented more fully the nature of her life as she acclimated to Los Angeles and motherhood. When Jacqueline first came to see me, she denied that the cocaine was an addiction. She felt it gave her the energy she needed to care for her family, while functioning as an artist. Besides, she wasn't a daily user, she reasoned. She could go weeks without it. One day, she came into the session bereft. She'd done something she had never done before. She'd gone to a seedy side of town to purchase her coke and had gone on a sort of bender, stopping only when it was completely gone. I told her it was time to stop kidding herself. She was not an occasional user. In that moment, she understood that however sporadic it was, she had a chemical dependency. Just then, a beautiful butterfly flew in an open window behind her head. I motioned for her to turn around to see it. I told her that she was the butterfly. Sometimes we must do something to an extreme before we can transform it. In admitting she had a problem, she'd taken the first step toward transformation.

Like a caterpillar that must first walk before it can fly, there was an opportunity to go into the cocoon of her unconscious and emerge with wings. Only this time, freedom would mean something much more profound than flying all over the world at a moment's whim. It would mean clearing the blocks of unworthiness she'd carried from childhood that were preventing her from being as powerful an artist, mother, and human being as possible.

The massive stone she was carving in her studio became very symbolic of her recovery process. She'd make progress and then she'd occasionally fall off the wagon, but when the piece was finished, she'd turned to her inner muse and spirit more often than not, finally coming to a peaceful place where her past became the material she used to recreate herself and her work.

Jacqueline began volunteering with inner-city kids, teaching them about art from other cultures. She assisted a nonprofit group dedicated to exposing kids to art by creating a studio where they could learn to draw and paint. As Jacqueline demonstrated, the key to minimizing relapse goes beyond merely being creative. It was motherhood that anchored her to one place long enough for her to delve more deeply into what she had been seeking through drugs. And it was motherhood that inspired her to place her role as an artist inside a bigger purpose. Through helping inner-city kids, Jacqueline began to believe she could play a modest role in making a better world for her children.

Having consulted for several chemical-dependency treatment centers, I believe that discovering one's soul purpose can be a very effective method for relapse prevention. If you have relapsed, it's very important to obtain help from someone who not only can assist you in getting back into abstinence, but who can also coach you to expand your efforts toward a new life that includes giving back to others.

As anyone in a recovery program knows, addictions keep us humble. However, should your LifeQuake involve addressing addictions (and everyone has at least one), it can provide you with the material for a deeper understanding of your mission. Whether or not you struggle with addictions, the only thing that ultimately will inspire you is calling on the Wholy Self to transform your feelings of defeat.

When we merge our awareness with that of the Wholy Self, we remember that we are, indeed, whole, already in our full potential. We are neither our addictions nor our seeming failures to succeed. Through commanding this merging, we become one again with all that is real. The mastery of stage five is your willingness to keep coming back to the road while it winds its way over rocky, uncharted territory, no matter how many times you've wandered into the forest. Obviously, it helps to be in great physical shape so let's talk about your health habits now.

Cauliflower, Chlorella, and Core Yoga

As your energy returns in stage five, you may be tempted to take on too many activities and thus neglect the inner world you traversed in stage four. The development of an inner life in stage four may have come out of being in transition and not having the new life to busy yourself in as you did before. Stage five's new opportunities may lead you to neglect your health in an effort to make up for time spent in the void of stage four. Even if you still have the same career, chances are there was a slowing down of your productivity in the previous stages, as your soul demanded an inward focus. Now that your energy has picked up, the key question is: How are you going to use it?

Sometimes in stage five, we return to the same work we were doing before, only in a restructured format. One of my clients entered stage four, in complete burnout from working as an executive in advertising. She'd developed a severe case of fibromyalgia and went on disability. After working with an acupuncturist, nutritionist, and me, she finally felt ready to work again. Initially, she didn't want to go back to the high-pressure world of advertising. In fact, she felt drawn to working with the elderly. During her stage four transition, her parents had each become ill, which led to her becoming well-versed in all services that support the elderly and their families. She became passionate about ways to help the aged population on how they could get complete care—from "soup to nuts." However, she didn't yet feel equipped to become an entrepreneur. Soon after, a freelance position opened up in advertising, one she decided to take. Not being in charge allowed her to work fewer hours; she also negotiated a deal where she could go into work later, allowing her to meditate in the morning, do core yoga to strengthen her gut, and cook a nutritious hot meal that she would take to work with her. Freelancing allowed her to make trips home to see her parents and spend time developing her consulting business for baby boomers with elderly parents.

A major key to building a foundation that allows you to be a master of change and adaptability is nutrition, which is why I emphasize it in previous stages. Food is a primary source for energy, but even healthy food is not assimilated the same for everyone. Healthy foods can still make you sick if your body is rejecting it through an allergy. Do you wake up in the morning in brain fog? Are you tired after a typical meal? You may have food allergies. It doesn't mean you have to give up that food for good. A good nutritionist will put you on an elimination diet and rotate the foods you should eat in and out of your weekly routine.

If you can't afford this consulting and testing, there are three things that Dr. Jacqueline Chan (author of *Regenerate Your Brain*, 2020) suggests for anyone in stage five: digestive enzymes, probiotics, and glutamine while paying attention to how you feel for the next couple hours after you eat.

"Digestive enzymes assist your stomach in breaking down the food you eat so it can be assimilated by your body. If you eat animal protein, you need one that has lipase and protease in it. If you are a dairy eater, it needs to also have lactase. And for starches, it needs to have amylase in it. Glutamine is an amino acid that treats inflammation in the bowel or leaky gut syndrome.

Probiotics consists of lactobacillus, bifidus, and other forms of healthy gut bacteria. Stress alone can kill off healthy bacteria in your gut, so it's a good idea when you're going through the transition into a more active life in stage five that you replenish your gut and assist its assimilation of the food you're ingesting. Assimilating food is how you get your energy. Remember, you need all the energy you can muster in this stage of rebuilding of your body and lifestyle. Building a healthy gut first, plays a critical role in balancing the nervous system snd supporting the immune system."

Because stage five is all about continually re-tooling your life so that the foundation you build is strong, I recommend recording in your journal how you feel physically at the end of each day. Notice the activities and foods you ate on days when you feel great, as well as on those days when you feel lethargic. Include any particular stressors that were present. At the end of every week, look at your notes and decide what needs to be eliminated and what needs to be enhanced. If you're not working with a doctor, engage the help of a friend to look at your journal. Perhaps you can do this for each other. This is how you sharpen your awareness and become more adept at foreseeing and adapting to change.

Workplace

Working in an environment that supports you is another critical brick in building a new foundation. Do you work with people who stimulate your creativity? Is it an environment that allows you to express your mission? How easy or difficult is it to maintain good health habits at your workplace? If you have been working from home alone, is that still supporting you or do you need to have other co-workers? If you answered no to at least two of these, you may need to reconsider and take action. Get clear about what you need from your work environment in order to thrive. If you're stuck in the conversation that says "I have no choice; this job pays the bills," you'll have a lot of ground to cover in stage five. Begin by identifying your specific needs and exploring activities, environments, and issues that pique your interest.

If you have a calling that people think is crazy, be willing to take responsibility for refining it so that you can be heard and understood.

When I asked Martin Rutte if he met with much resistance when he talked about spirituality in corporate environments, he explained that initially his clients opposed the idea, claiming that spirituality had no place in business. "They were afraid it was going to cause disruption in the business. So we got around that by being very respectful and by showing the benefits," he explained. Rutte did his homework, researching the needs of his clients, not in books or statistics but on the ground, by talking to employees. "People were afraid that I was going to proselytize. They thought I was coming in with a particular view of how spirituality in the workplace should look." To get around this objection, he began to ask people a simple question: What would it be like if you were fully present to your work and had good communication with your employees on any issue? As the inquiry took off and Rutte saw its positive effects, he began to use the word "beingness" to describe this down-to-earth human quality that he helped people cultivate in their workplace. Martin softened people's resistance by meeting it with respect and non-judgment. He enjoyed the challenge and seized the opportunity to introduce a new paradigm in the workplace.

One of my clients had enjoyed a very lucrative career as a voice-over actor on a major television network. For years, he'd worked a four-hour workday and was much more involved in his children's lives than the average dad. When he turned forty though, his contract wasn't renewed, so the network put him on-call to be brought in as needed.

He'd started to feel lackluster about his job about a year before all this transpired and was even depressed from time to time. His original plan in moving to Hollywood had been to pursue film acting, and although he made a good living, he wasn't challenged by voice-over work any longer. He needed to stretch creatively but had become unmotivated while committed to a long-term contract. He'd been playing around with photography for years, but never saw it as a viable profession. With his world thrown up for grabs, he took a first step by reorganizing the family garage and creating a dark room and workspace. He continued doing voice-over work while developing a photography portfolio. I encouraged him to write a soul purpose statement and then a mission statement. He took on the challenge and, in the process, discovered his deepest desire was to be an independent film director and began producing and directing short films in stage five.

The important lesson to take from this story has to do with claiming and clearing the space for your vocation to emerge. Find a place in your apartment or house that is to be used solely for the purpose of working on your mission, even if it's just a corner of your bedroom or a space on the dining room table. Then, spend time there for at least 30 minutes a day.

Relationships

In stage four, I encouraged you to experiment with relationships, to meet new people you might not ordinarily be drawn to in order to experience who the new you might be attracted to. In stage five, as you're drawing the ever-changing blueprint, the key is to be clear about your values. What are your must-haves in a relationship? What is negotiable? The biggest mistake people make is confusing these two concepts. What is non-negotiable for you, in both a mate and a friend? Sometimes these issues are subtle. For example, let's say respect is non-negotiable for you. How do you gauge respect? Someone may love you dearly but have trouble keeping his word. How important is that value to you? How do you feel after you see someone? Are you energized or drained by his or her company.

If you're still married or in a long-term relationship in stage five, your values and/or interests may have changed since your relationship first began. It may be time to consciously redesign the relationship contract. Sit down with your partner and make a list of your must-haves. Keep it short and simple. Now, discuss your lists. Is there a big difference in your values and priorities? How do you reconcile the differences? Now that you're clear about having a life purpose and mission, is your mate interested in creating a mission statement for the relationship? How important is that to you? It may be helpful to arrange an appointment with a marriage or relationship therapist to discuss how you can build a relationship that is firmly aligned with your life purpose and mission. If the two of you find you're not on the same page, evaluate whether the relationship can transition into a new form. Can it work more authentically as a friendship or professional partnership? I encourage working with a counselor whose objectivity can help you redefine the relationship.

Support Groups

As you let go of people and relationships that no longer fit you in stage three or four, you may want to look for a support group or group coaching of some kind. Joining a group can help you develop healthier, more authentic relationships. Here, you learn the building block of humility by asking for help from a group of new friends. However, it needs to be the right fit. If you get involved in charity organizations, church groups, or an anonymous group that addresses addictions, notice how you feel after you leave. If it doesn't feel like they mirror your core values, remember the *Magna Doodle* or *Etch A Sketch* exercise. Simply wipe that particular group off the blueprint and try another.

Some organizations will actually help you get clear about your calling. For one client, *Toastmasters International* played an important role. That organization has a clear mission: "To help men and women learn the arts of speaking, listening, and thinking—vital skills that promote self-actualization, enhance leadership, foster human understanding, and contribute to the betterment of mankind." My client had been a fifth grade school teacher who entered stage four with a back injury. While on disability, she realized she still loved to teach, but in order to avoid back surgery, she would need to find a venue for her talents that didn't require being on her feet six hours a day, five days a week. Through Toastmasters, she got clear that she wanted to become a keynote speaker and workshop leader for conferences devoted to education. This would allow her to be on her feet for only a few hours, twice a month. Because public speaking pays much more than teaching, she didn't have to work standing up full time. As many professional speakers will tell you, 75 percent of their work is on the phone, getting the gigs.

Finding the right kind of group support is very dependent on the specifics of your LifeQuake. Most can be found online now. For example, if you contracted breast cancer in stage three, after your physical healing process is complete in stage four, you may need a breast cancer survivors group. Studies show that survival rates of those women who attend a support group for just an hour once a week in the year following their surgery are significantly higher than those who don't. Once you've settled into personal group support, then it may be appropriate to join other groups that have a training capacity, like Toastmasters or

Zoom classes designed to assist you in discovering and actuating your soul purpose.

Accidental Power

My own experience of accidents is that they often aren't so accidental. As I mentioned in earlier chapters, they often carry a message. After a horseback riding accident left her bedridden for a year, Janet was rebuilding her career as a college professor at the time she came to see me. She offered that she was writing a book, a textbook that she'd been commissioned to write by a publisher. I pushed, "There is another book within you, one that is more personal and creative," I asserted. She admitted that she indeed had an idea for a book. This one was on creativity and was based on some of her life experiences as a recovering alcoholic. I encouraged her to take notes on this book while she wrote the other one. She admitted to feeling a great deal of fear about writing this other book.

We began to explore how she could tap into the universal source for energy, rather than depleting her adrenals glands. We worked to open and clear her crown chakra to allow the light of the super-conscious mind to feed her muse and give her inspiration. We also worked with her dreams, which indicated that she was being initiated into a new source of creative power. At one point in our work, she became conflicted about this. I asked her to identify her deepest fear. She revealed a dread that is almost universal: "If I fully step into my power, others will become less powerful as a result." Rather than confront this belief as irrational, I gave her an assignment to write a dialogue between herself and the power. I suggested she allow her rational mind to write with her dominant hand, expressing its fears and questions. Then she was to write with her non-dominant hand, allowing her intuitive, powerful self to respond. When we spoke again, it was clear that reconciliation had occurred between her two aspects.

As you build your new inner and outer foundation, if you have issues with being powerful, you'll need to confront those limiting beliefs. In your old worldview, you may have perceived power as a benefit that came with success in your career or marital status, your net worth, family background or even your fitness level. Now, in stage five, power begins to take on a deeper meaning. For me, it grew out of my smile that came from my heart. A radiant smile in my interactions with others was a powerful force that forwarded their light as well.

Building Elements

The building elements in stage five are *inspiration, persistence, and humility.* You cross a threshold of maturity when inspiration replaces ambition as the fuel for your life. That's not to say you lose your ambition, just that your center of gravity shifts from I-me-mine to "How can I best serve the larger whole?" In the face of challenges, you learn to persist. You understand that the bigger picture is a work in progress. Using intuitive discretion, you learn to ask for help from the right people. This is humility in action; it stems from the wisdom of knowing you can't do it alone. The cycle of giving and receiving becomes alive in you as you gain a healthy sense of interdependence. You also learn yet another aspect of adaptability: the discernment of knowing when to act and when to retreat, when to persist and when to change direction.

As in all the stages, it's important to affirm that these elements are being anchored into your subconscious and conscious mind. Further, by calling on the Wholy Self (which is a form of the unified field of consciousness) you anchor these elements more rapidly and attract like-minded individuals. Here is an example of this invocation: "I now call in the radiant light of unconditional love and receive the assistance of all those who come from this vibration. I am now filled with the building elements of *inspiration, persistence,* and *humility.* Thank you." Feel your sense of self, expanding beyond your body. As you let go of your former identity, experimenting as a beginner dissolves old boundaries of who you were into this bigger field where possibilities are limitless.

The Toolbox

Taking the "Fault" Out of the Faulty Foundation

Thomas Edison once said, "I have not failed. I have discovered twelve hundred ideas that don't work." Edison's wisdom teaches us to see undesirable results as part of a learning curve, rather than as failures. This attitude requires two key attributes: *humility* and *persistence.* To best develop these qualities, we do well to clear out the past and let go of whatever residual disappointment, shame, or self-doubt we may be carrying, both consciously and unconsciously.

Before embarking on a new project, call in The Wholy Self and the violet flame that was introduced in stage two. Close your eyes and invite them both to surround your body. With your intention and your breath, release into the violet flame every belief both known and unknown, that causes you to quit too soon. Release into the violet flame your entire past up until this moment. Let go of all interpretations of what success and failure mean. Imagine a clean slate. See the name of your next project on the slate. Once you feel you're truly ready to be completely present in this moment, imagine yourself as Whole -y, your fullest potential standing in front of you. This version of you already exists in a parallel universe. This is an exercise that gives you access to quantum reality where this you is here now, outside of linear time. From this place, it is possible to collapse time and bring that more evolved you from another dimension into this body.

What qualities does this person have that you think you lack? For example, you might see this "future you" as having great enthusiasm in the face of a breakdown, or as being able to maintain inspiration and focus throughout the ups and downs of every phase of a project, from creation to marketing. Allow the old concept of the present you to merge with the quantum you, and feel the joy this brings into your body. Repeat this activation of the part of you who knows how to do this: "I begin again, knowing that everything is working for my highest and greatest good." Ask the Wholy Self to fuel your persistence with the inspiration of contributing to others through your projects or new vocation. Experience the you that has both the humility and faith to keep starting over.

Developmental Steps to Change Mastery

- ✓ Embrace the attitude of novice or student in acquiring new skills to implement your calling.

- ✓ Reframe setbacks as progressive approximations to manifesting your new life.

- ✓ Ask for assistance from others to actuate your vision.

- ✓ Write a mission statement.

- ✓ Design a new blueprint for your ideal life.

- ✓ Continually adapt the blueprint to fit the changing needs of an agile, mobile inner home.

Out of Manure Comes Harvest:
The How-To of True Wealth

There are two ways to live: you can live as if nothing is a miracle or you can live as though everything is a miracle.

~ Albert Einstein, pioneering quantum physicist

Onset

Stage six begins the minute you really understand that your thoughts and emotions manifest your outer reality. You can manifest abundance from the old paradigm of Newtonian physics that requires hard work and an "outside in" philosophy of reality: what you see outside of you is what you believe is true. Or, you can change your thoughts so they reflect the reality you want to create by acting as if the abundance you want has already manifested. This requires stepping out of your former identity into the quantum field where there are unlimited possibilities for creating what you want. Further, changing how you interpret the world brings prosperity from everything. This stage is devoted to developing the practices and consciousness that allows you to own this.

My favorite story about this distinction tells of the father who takes his twin sons down to the stables. He tells the boys that the stables are empty and sends each one into his own vacant stall, telling them to come back with a report on what they see. The first boy comes back looking disappointed. He reports that he found nothing but hay and horse manure in the stall. The second boy doesn't come back for quite some time, so the father goes into the stall to see what's caused his delay. He finds the boy digging through the haystack, piling hay and manure up into one corner of the stall. When he asks his son what he's doing, the boy exclaims, "There's manure everywhere, so there's gotta' be a pony in here somewhere!" (My version is a little cleaner than the original.)

You enter stage six when the meaning of "what you see is what you get" becomes "how you see is what you get." You've probably explored the idea that perception influences your experience of the world. In stage six this insight becomes a living truth.

Manure is just manure; the mind turns it into fertilizer or toxic waste. Nothing "out there" is a threat, except as your perception turns it into one. It's up to each of us to interpret the manure in our lives or from the latest global crisis as either bad news, which means no gain, or good news, which means we're on fertile ground. Henry Ford said it this way: "If you think you can or you think you can't, either way, you're right." Lest you think the "there's a pony in here somewhere" types are blind optimists, let's look a little closer. There is a big difference between blind optimism and what really is happening at this stage.

But first we'll take a peek at what it looks like at this point in your LifeQuake.

What It Looks Like

To master stage six, your insides and outsides must become more congruent. The sharp contrast between how you show up in the world and who you truly are, dissolves. The tools and teachings here are designed to help you do just that. Mastery comes from being more relaxed now inside your own skin and far more concerned with your well being than your image. Inwardly, you are achieving some sense of balance. You're conscious of your feelings, aware of your thoughts, and intentional in your focus. You're becoming more and more aligned with your soul purpose and have a sense that you're contributing to the greater good. Your enthusiasm is back; in certain moments, you're filled with authentic joy and gratitude.

You're beginning to understand the paradox of apparent loss and authentic gain. You have first hand experience of painful changes that lead to something unforeseen, even delightful, right around the corner. You recognize that you can experience life as filled with grace or fraught with struggle. You've developed an adaptability muscle; painful experiences need no longer take up permanent real estate in your mind and block you from seeing opportunity. You're putting your blueprint into action, and you've learned to keep adjusting your vision. Now, the master architect within is directing you, moment to moment.

The mastery at the end of this stage comes when you find it easy to think of yourself as prosperous, no matter what your external circumstances. Life is becoming rich once again. You feel wealthy, and your life shows up for you as one of prosperity. What is fundamental to this stage is your commitment to your soul purpose as the source of your wealth, regardless of your actual income. In the early stages of your LifeQuake, your perceptions about how your life looks were, in part, shaped by family, cultural values, and the matrix perpetrated by broadcast media and the Internet. Now, in stage six, the opportunity is to experience wealth independent of your bank balance or other defunct criteria. Your views about your life are meant to be informed by your heart as the leader, with your brain following orders. Clearing away old cultural programs and your former identity in stages 4 and 5 allows you to truly know what is being guided by your soul purpose. Again, because this model is non-linear, you may experience aspects of previous stages as you master this one.

What Is Really Happening

Because conventional values and opinions no longer govern your viewpoint, you can master the ability to hold the tension of opposites: what your negative ego would have you believe versus what the Wholy Self presents to your awareness. These two coexist along parallel tracks in your mind, no longer on a collision course of self-defeating behavior. You can make space for the negative voices that still pop up from time to time, and you know to call on the vastness of the Wholy Self to adjust your thoughts and vision. In other words, you're increasingly able to see the glass as more than half full. This isn't blind optimism; it's 'possibility thinking,' the ability to constructively co-exist with ambiguity while appreciating a good paradox.

Webster's Dictionary defines paradox as something that is contrary to or conflicts with conventional opinion. The ability to hold the constant paradox of life is the sign of a mind primed for wealth consciousness, what I like to call the *fertile soul*. Interestingly enough, Roget's Thesaurus offers the word fertile as a synonym for wealthy. In common use, fertile refers to soil that is rich in nutrients. To return once again to our earth metaphor, by stage six you're replacing layers of defunct cultural programming (the matrix) that kept you afraid of making changes with layers of new, rich soil. Obstacles, old ways of seeing the world, outdated identities—these become compost to enrich and fertilize your spirit. Now that the layers around your core aren't hard and encrusted, the soil moves more readily to reveal messages coming up from your soul. You don't need to be hit with catastrophic eruptions to get your attention, and if catastrophe does strike, you don't interpret it from the old default programming that insists that loss is bad.

When the Great Depression hit, some people jumped out of windows, while others saw financial opportunity inside of desperate economic times. Not just the wealthy got wealthier. What most people who prospered during the Depression had in common with each other was that they'd weathered other down times. They understood the nature of cycles so they didn't buy into the media's interpretation of the economy. They had fertile minds and could see the opportunity below the ground when, on the surface, the stock market crash appeared to be a catastrophic loss.

By now, you are building a foundation that can adapt more easily to change, even radical change, because nothing is perceived as permanent. Every day is a blank slate on which your blueprint is refined and further developed. If you do the work of ancestral deprogramming from stage four and the evening download from stage one, you needn't be impeded by the past as you embrace each new day. The beauty of this model is that if fear comes up, you can return to exercises and utilize them to clear any blocks or old beliefs that still arise and obstruct your way.

Mastering stage six requires your experience of success and failure to continually be redefined. You no longer judge yourself harshly when you've aspired to a certain goal that you don't quite reach. Likewise with success—it takes its rightful place in the larger scheme of things and no longer puts you on a lofty ego-boosting pedestal from which you could fall later on. You experience a new kind of abundance. You see that grace touches every aspect of life, no matter what results your efforts deliver.

The lesson of stage six is to engage in thought patterns that keep your spirit fertile, even in the face of both anticipated and unexpected change. Therefore, as you intuit that your blueprint needs altering to live more authentically, or you're confronted with a sudden loss, the key is to persist in perceiving your life as having a purpose. A certain lightness of being accompanies the process of change.

Fertility Versus the Futility of Loss

Like a cat with nine lives, I became a little savvier with each brush with death. It took me nearly a year to get firmly back on my feet after my first nearly fatal encounter with a skid-row addict strung out on PCP. Seven years later, after my week of car accidents, I also went into a protracted recovery period. Both incidents were extremely traumatic and involved a slow recovery period, and on both occasions, I was even forced to stop working for a time. More relevant here, however, is that I suffered emotionally because my interpretation of both experiences rendered me a victim. That all changed with my third near-demise ...

I'd been sick for months; doctors suspected it was my thyroid. The medication they prescribed wired me up, leaving me exhausted. Having learned not to resist fatigue, I spent a lot of time resting. In my constant state of repose, the stillness revealed that my life was changing and a transition had begun. I didn't know how it would manifest, but I knew that change was coming.

When my body broke out in a rash, I went to see my acupuncturist. She noticed a metallic odor when she inserted the acupuncture needles and told me to look for an environmental cause. Immediately, I thought about the small spots that'd recently started to form on my linoleum. I talked to my landlord, who casually remarked that the previous tenant had complained of black mold and moved out, but that he had removed it with bleach before I had moved in. I hired an environmental consultant who came out and took samples. Before he left, I asked him what he thought it was, totally unprepared for the wrecking ball that had already been set in motion.

"I can't be sure until I test these samples in the lab," he said, "but I believe this is Stachybotrys Chartarum, the deadliest mold there is."

When I explained that I'd been ill, he looked me in the eye and said, "This stuff kills people, lady. If I were you, I'd move out today." "What about my belongings?" I probed.

"Anything in the house that cannot be put through 50% bleach has to go or hire a mold remediation company but they are very expensive." My landlord refused to pay for mold remediation so I had to make the hard decision and fast.

When I walked out of the house two hours later, I left everything behind—I had no choice. Inexplicably, I had a feeling that my soul was testing my resistance to change, and I was determined to pass the test this time. I declared that I would hold the faith and enter a new, more authentic life, even if it meant giving up everything I had owned.

I left my home with only the clothes on my back, and while I would love to say that I was able to keep the faith during my two-month stay in a motel, I did get unhinged at times. Eating in cheap restaurants three times a day, sleep deprivation caused by noisy motel customers, and my body weakened even further by detoxing, brought me to my knees more than once. As my story illustrates, we can pop in and out of change mastery, so it's very important to be compassionate and self-accepting when you aren't joyful or enthusiastic. The key is staying true to your feelings and dropping into them with your breath, rather than running from your emotions.

Sometimes during times of great transition, the only emotionally honest practice is to acknowledge what is working and yet also create an inner container for all the emotions based in resistance to come up and be held by your witness self. This was my lifeline while living in the motel. On a daily basis, I acknowledged the grace, even when I didn't want to. When we're confronted with a situation that seems like pure manure, the real lesson comes in keeping the faith until that damn pony can be found!

During my two months of temporary housing, I began to love having my room cleaned and my bed made by the housekeeper every day. I delighted in the fact that my car stayed clean under a covered parking garage, and that practically everything I wore was brand new. Of course, negative thoughts came up as well. I got plenty of practice facing my dualistic thinking and even started playing with imaginary cartoon characters to embody the paradox. My negative ego was a little devil on one shoulder. In my imagination, I would send this little 'toon into the room next door with a roll of duct tape to cover the mouth of the guy with a relentless cough. I chose not to fuel my dark thoughts with judgments, so I'd observe my mind, laugh out loud, and then breathe into my homicidal fantasies until they passed.

Owning the selves in the Cellar (stage four's lesson) can keep you honest and free of shame when the challenges get too great. Someone sent me a quote that ran through my head when I needed to regain my sense of humor: "Angels can fly because they take themselves lightly." I had to learn to take other people lightly, too.

Let the Good Times Roll

Typically, we are most observant of our spiritual practices when we're uncertain, scared, or in a crisis. Part of maintaining stage-six awareness is never taking for granted what's working. When you acknowledge everything, from getting a good parking space to having a roof over your head, you develop the muscle of gratitude. This makes it easier to see grace, even when life serves up difficulties.

When a client comes to a session and reports that there is nothing to talk about because the week went so well, I have him or her review the week, listing all the support that may have gone unnoticed or unacknowledged. When a breakdown occurs, or we make a mistake, we analyze it to death. We coulda', shoulda', woulda' done things differently, and others involved coulda', shoulda', woulda' done things differently, too. Let's apply this same scrutiny to what you do right. Take the time to analyze what contributed to the good week, rather than pass it off as luck or coincidence.

Humorous Health Prescriptions

During my time when all of what was comforting and familiar was simply gone, I kept a journal of everything that was funny or amusing. For example, my blood test came back to reveal that I had inhaled heavy doses of black mold and a few other neurotoxins that were found in the house. The doctor gave me a list of foods that I should and shouldn't eat while my immune system was so compromised. I looked at the list and joked, "Are grapes okay, particularly the fermented ones?" She said quite seriously, "I wouldn't suggest drinking wine, but vodka is perfectly fine." I left her office, went straight to P.F. Chang's around the corner, and had two Greyhound cocktails. I figured I was killing two birds with one stone since grapefruit juice contains vitamin C.

Not a big drinker, I indeed got pleasantly high on my "health tonics." The irony of my new food plan was that I'd stopped eating the very thing vodka is made from—potatoes—because they have gluten in them. In my mold-clogged mind, I figured if the doctor said it was okay, then it must be okay, especially in a liquid state. The next morning, I woke up with a hangover that pushed me right back on the wagon. The incident was one of the few humorous moments I managed to extract from many frustrating visits to doctors who didn't know how to treat mold contamination.

If you get anything from this chapter, let it be this: if you choose to experience yourself as being wealthy, it doesn't matter what your life looks like on the outside.

Candles in the Dark

Anne left her husband and an Italian villa-like home on the water to move into a tiny two-bedroom apartment with her two children. Listen to her tell the story: "Unbeknownst to me, he had siphoned all of our money into offshore holdings. His story was that his clothing manufacturing business had gone bankrupt. I left him the day I got a call from a scorned lover who informed me to the contrary. I had stayed with him through his infidelities and supposed money problems in the past because I feared being a single mother with my two kids in an apartment. My fear became a self-fulfilling prophecy. What I didn't count on was that this little apartment would become a miniature castle, a comforting fortress for me as I transitioned into my new life. What turned my life around outwardly was that in spite of cherishing the home I had left, I didn't identify who I was anymore with my circumstances. What I would have considered constraint and confinement in the past became ease and manageability—in a word, cozy. Rituals that gave me pleasure helped: lighting candles, making nourishing soups, and keeping our tiny home filled with fresh flowers. All of these inexpensive indulgences really fed my soul."

Anne added, "Bring things back into simplicity. Order in your home makes a big difference. Continually get rid of everything that doesn't work with your life. Have you worn that blue sweater in the last year? Improving your home life demonstrates how outer transformation can create inner transformation. As a result of limited finances and living in smaller quarters, my children and I grew closer. We all sat on the same sofa and watched one television and ate at home together more often.

Cultivate gratitude. Be in a constant dialogue with God. Part of wealth consciousness for me was also telling the truth. It's okay to say "I'm having a bad day" and yet not have it define me. In the old days, I thought I always had to put on a happy face or people wouldn't like me. Now I don't care, and the irony is I'm the person everybody trusts to be real."

It took four years and an expensive lawsuit to recover her half of the community property. Of equal import—and particularly rewarding for Anne was that her case set a precedent that will make it easier for women to advance their claims in the Cayman Islands. Anne's Life-Quake led to the discovery of a new mission to teach women (particularly housewives) to be brave in their lives and face the truth of what is really going on in their marriage and to make sure their assets are managed properly. If your intuition tells you that the person taking care of your money—whether a husband, an accountant, or a broker—is not on the level, listen and take action. Part of being a fertile soul means taking responsibility for the income and outgo of your financial resources.

Anne also went on to form a company that produces candles (the very thing that provided comfort in her darkest moments) and donates a percentage to causes that support women.

Time-Outs That Replenish

Once you're doing work you love, you still need time-outs. As a kid, being sent to your room for a time-out was a drag. Who knew time alone in your room would one day feel like a vacation? My clients love to tell me they have no time for themselves; I agree with them. Argue for your limitations, and they're yours. You may be successful in the way the world defines success, but if you can't take time out every day to just daydream or meditate, something is dead wrong, and you will not be able to master wealth consciousness.

I find music to be a great accessory to a time-out. Choose selections that elevate your spirit. What are the songs that make you happy and move you to sing along? I love Italian ballads such as *Volare*, *Al Di La*, and *Arrivederci Roma*. Singing them expands my energy and puts me right back into a fertile soul when I have fallen into a slump. Find music that makes you want to dance; then make a mood-elevating play list that you can turn on any time you lose your edge.

Dancing is another way to get back to an ebullient state. Jules Pfeiffer created Pulitzer Prize-winning comic strips of characters dancing to tragic feeling states or events. If anger is something stuck in your body and you're having trouble maintaining a fertile soul, honor it by dancing the emotion through. Find music that evokes that specific feeling. If you're angry, you might choose hard rock, heavy metal, or hip-hop songs. When you're really expressing yourself through vigorous movement, the energy will lighten by the time the song is over. Music is incredibly healing when used in this way. It is also a great ally to shifting your heart back into coherence with what you want to create. It will carry you back into the Quantum Field where you can envision what you do want from an elevated mood state.

Your head can readily turn into a bad neighborhood when you encounter tough times. So get out of your head and into nature. If you live in the city and can't get out of the hustle and bustle until the weekend, do a five-minute closed-eye visualization. Do you remember a special place where the natural world filled you with awe and a sense of peace? Imagine that place in as much detail as possible and tap into the Wholy Self for direction. Ask what step needs to be taken. Often, just taking the next right action will get you unstuck and back in your groove.

Pagliacci Is a Blonde

Some people have a hard time moving into stage six. For Diane Miller, who you first met in chapter two, this was certainly the case. At the end of her Cosmic Barbeque, Diane discovered her next mission in life: to help victims of domestic violence. But she toiled for years in stage five.

Diane's work with Court Watch, the nonprofit she founded in 1992, brought about many changes to the law in California. Today's woman has far more legal protection than Diane had when her husband threatened her life in the late 1970's. Diane found it difficult to ask for money and as a consequence, Court Watch operated on a shoestring for years. Relying on contributions, donated space, hand-me-down office equipment, and a trickle of volunteers, Diane did the work she truly believed in and successfully led the crusade. But prosperity consciousness eluded her—until the day she got notice from her landlord that Court Watch was about to be evicted. Finally, Diane dug in and did the work of stage six and uncovered her blocks to prosperity.

The first was an old belief from her parents that cash is in limited supply. Diane always had enough for the essentials—food, clothing, and a lovely home, but her belief system prevented her from having more than she needed to cover the basics. Perhaps this arose from her Roman Catholic roots, coupled with a semiconscious belief that humanitarians had to take the vow of poverty. But an even more elusive block was revealed when Diane realized she'd lost her sense of humor.

Prior to founding Court Watch, Diane had always seen herself as a bit like Pagliacci, the clown and lead character in the opera of the same name. Like Pagliacci, Diane always managed to laugh on the outside, even while crying within. Diane's sense of humor had always been her greatest salvation in tough times. But working with the tragedy of so many women's lives, she had lost that Pagliacci edge.

Diane's breakthrough came when she followed the advice of a workshop leader and took a "money bath". As per instructions, Diane borrowed a thousand dollars, converted it into one-dollar bills and spread the money across her bed. She then sat in the middle of the bed and rubbed the money all over her body, throwing it up into the air like a little kid. Diane even did a fan dance with the money to really make it fun. This clever intervention allowed her to unravel the notion that being nonprofit literally meant making no profit! Moreover, it helped her resurrect her sense of humor and infuse her beliefs about money with joy. "I understood what true abundance could feel like," she remembered.

When I asked Diane what had changed, she explained, "I just got lighter about it, and the miracles began to happen. First, a benefactor came in and donated an office. Then a woman senator invited me to attend a weekend gathering in Northern California. Before I did that money bath exercise, I would've declined, thinking I couldn't afford a weekend away at this time in my life. But I listened to the small voice inside that told me to go. That weekend, I met the Minister of Education and several other dignitaries from Bermuda; they were there to conduct a fact-finding mission. Their goal was to create a computer science curriculum for the public schools. I offered a few ideas and suggestions, and they asked me on the spot if I would take it on. Then came the turning point when they popped the big question and asked about my fee. To my surprise, the words 'ten thousand dollars a month' just rolled off my tongue. That was twenty years ago. Since learning to manifest through the Quantum Field, unblocked by old beliefs, money comes easily to me now." Taking a break, even when we're doing work we love, can lend a larger perspective that expands our world. As the case above illustrates, that leap of faith can bring a new vocation at an even far-reaching level.

Wealthy Spirit

Chellie Campbell is the total embodiment of what she calls the wealthy spirit. Her book by the same title has helped thousands of readers reduce financial stress. The following excerpt from *The Wealthy Spirit* is her personal story, as told in the chapter titled: "Sometimes You Have to Ask God for a Sign."

For months, my agent, Lisa Hagan, and I searched for a publisher for this book. Many rejections and several almost-deals later, I still didn't have one. At one time, I had a deal with Harper/San Francisco. They had a series of books in a page-a-day format, like *365 Dao*, *365 Goddess*, etc., and thought my page-a-day format about money would really fit in with that. I was so excited! I celebrated, called all my friends, announced it at my Le Tip breakfast, and everyone cheered for my success. Four days later, they canceled the deal because their parent company, Harper Collins in New York, had just signed another person's page-a-day money book. So not only had I lost the deal, someone else had developed my same idea and was going to be the first one to market with it. I was just destroyed over it … for a day or two. And then I decided that no way could this other woman write *my* book because *my* book was *my* story of *my* life, and no one else could do that. And I got back to work and back to practicing my positive publishing affirmations, for example: "My book is a NY Times Bestseller, helps many people, inspires and entertains readers, and easily makes me rich and famous.". I remembered that God has three answers to prayers: Yes, not now, and I have something better for you. I knew that my book was good. I knew I could write, and I knew in my bones I would find a publisher. Okay, not this one. Jack Canfield told me the four-letter word to use when someone rejects you: "Next!" I wouldn't give up.

There are times you have to decide when to hold 'em and when to fold 'em. You fold 'em when you feel finished, when you no longer have passion for the work, when you don't see that other people are benefiting from your work. You fold 'em when the price tag is too high and the rewards not good enough. But you hold on when you love what you do, when you believe in yourself, when others believe in you and benefit from your work. Delay is not defeat. When the world crushes you and it all gets too hard, you get in bed, turn the electric blanket up to mother, and eat chocolate. But only do it for a day. Then remember that people are praying for you to show up and help them, and then you get up and help them. And by helping them, you help yourself.

Meanwhile, a friend from my writers group had the most glorious success. Rhonda Britten prepared her proposal, met with nine publishers, her book went up for auction, and she got a six-figure advance! I was truly happy for her and celebrated her success. But I couldn't help asking God, "Hey, what about me?"

I was willing to do whatever it took to get a publisher. Lisa told me that most of the publishers disliked the original page-a-day structure. So I revised the proposal and rewrote the book as an eight-chapter narrative. I changed the packaging and paid to have a matching cover design for my audio and videotapes. The new packages went out to publishers, and once again, Lisa and I waited.

Meanwhile, I had a conversation with God. I asked God for a sign. I told Him I have done everything I knew how to do, and now I needed Him to clearly show me if this goal, this book, was meant for me or not. I let Him know that I am here to do His work, and that I was willing to get my poor human ego out of the way and give this up, if that was what He wanted me to do. But I needed a clear sign whether or not to keep trying.

Exactly two days later, Deb Werksman at Sourcebooks called to say she was interested in my book. We discussed the narrative version and then she asked, "What's this page-a-day book that your agent told me about? She says everyone in her office uses it." After I described it to her, she said, "I want to see that book." It wasn't long before I got another call from her: "I just got out of an acquisitions meeting. We would love to publish your book!"

And you know what? They bought the original version!

God's on duty, 24/7. He's just waiting for you to ask. *The Wealthy Spirit* sold so many copies over a three-year period that Chellie's publisher asked her to write a second book. Sourcebooks published *Zero to Zillionaire* in April 2006 and *From Worry to Wealthy: A Woman's Guide to Financial Success Without the Stress* in 2015. For more information on Chellie's work, go to **chellie.com**

Chellie is a master of persistence, patience, and perseverance— stage-five's building elements. Her story exemplifies these qualities and offers several important lessons that bear repeating here. First, allow yourself to be guided by a clear mission, even while the specifics of its unfolding continually morph into new form. Second, keep turning within as you take your work to the next level. Third, ask to be shown the purpose of seeming disappointments. The Wholy Self will give you an answer far beyond how the ego might interpret it, and if you don't get a clear message, do what Chellie does: ask for a sign.

Changing Your Story

I interviewed Tama Kieves, like myself a career transitions expert, because her story is compelling. She is the bestselling author of *This Time I Dance! Creating the Work You Love, Thriving Through Uncertainty, Inspired & Unstoppable: Wildly Succeeding in Your Life's Work!* and *A Year without Fear: 365 Days of Magnificence*. She is also an honors graduate of Harvard Law who left the partnership track of a prestigious law firm to write and help others discover the life they were born to live.

Tama elaborates, " I was desperate to be free, exhausted in my good, safe job that was suffocating the life out of my creative soul. Finally, a friend asked me a vital question:

"If you're this successful doing work you *don't* love, what could you do with work you *do* love?"

I decided to answer that question with my life. I left the practice of law to undergo the art, practice, and baptism of listening to myself in this lifetime. These days I am on the faculty of the Omega Institute, Esalen, 1440, and other holistic venues. I've also been featured on Oprah radio, ABC News, the Huffington Post, Success Magazine and other national media.

As you can see, none of that would have been possible if Tama had not been willing to defy her Jewish roots for what defined success.

Here is one exercise from Tama's work called, *Writing Inspired Self Dialogues:*

The most generous and useful thing you can do for yourself is "talk" to your Inspired Self. Challenges will arise. Moods will flag. But you don't have to let a funky energy take over your perspective and possibilities. It's so important to diffuse your fear and open to your love. Remember, you *always* have an inspired way to see everything in your life.

Write to Your Inner Teacher, the wise one, the Advocate, your Beloved, your Success Coach Extraordinaire, God, Spirit, a cool figment of your imagination, a better figment than your fear. You may feel like you're "making it up" initially. Keep going. It works. This Voice has saved my life. Follow these four steps:

1. When you're in fear, write your concerns in detail to your Inspired Self. Be honest. You don't need to stay polite here or stay positive. Share your real feelings.

2. Let your Inspired Self write back to you and answer you. Your Inspired Self is the most loving and powerful and on-your-side voice you can possibly imagine. Some of you may have religious/spiritual beliefs to draw on. For some, your Loving Voice may be the voice of God, Jesus, Krishna, or an Angel. For others, this voice may be the voice of a nurturing parent, grandmother, friend or lover. For years, I've called my voice Inner Teacher, then shortened it to Teacher. Sometimes the best way to access this voice is to think: What would I say to

my best friend or my child---someone who I wanted the best for in life? Let *that* Presence answer the fear.

3. Dialogue back and forth-until you feel peace.

4. When you start you may feel as though you are "making this up." It may feel awkward. I don't care. Do it anyway. The more you do this practice, the more this voice will become real to you. It's life changing wisdom…and you have it at your fingertips.

For more information on the work of Tama Kieves, visit the following website: **www.TamaKieves.com**

Just as you worked to "rewrite" the story of your childhood in chapter four, here you are rewriting your story about the current challenges, infusing that interpretation with passion and success. This is the fertile soul in action, turning the manure into a rich and satisfying life.

A Global LifeQuake

In the first decade of this century we encountered national disasters like Hurricane Katrina and Wall Street quakes that triggered global economic crisis. In the second decade, we began to address the climate crisis as a shared global challenge but not quickly enough. Now in this third decade, we are confronting through pandemics that trigger global economic crisis, the negative effects that insufficient personal health habits and poverty may have on the immune system. It is my vision that part of developing the fertile soul in mass consciousness will further connect the link between each person taking responsibility for reducing their carbon footprint and enhancing their immune system as part of a long-term strategy for healing the planet. We will take a deeper dive on this in chapter seven.

Staying out of all of the various media's matrix of doom and gloom may not be easy but it is fundamental to maintaining a *fertile soul* and, as Chellie Campbell calls it, a Wealthy Spirit.

So, let's journey back to the first global crisis that defined the 21st century. The day after the World Trade Center attacks on 9/11, I began putting together a workshop to address what was clearly a nationwide crisis. Although I was extremely fatigued and still didn't know why, I felt very strongly that our country and possibly the world was beginning a LifeQuake. I intuited that this crisis was the tip of an iceberg whose effects would last throughout the first decade.

The parallels to my personal LifeQuake were uncanny. My discovery that my house and body were contaminated came exactly a month later. While living in a motel, I was truly given an opportunity for quickening into a fertile soul. Could I execute my mission while living in these circumstances? Stage three had hit the country on a massive scale, and I needed to do my part, sudden move or not.

The obstacles were daunting: all my paperwork had been contaminated, not to mention my answering machine, computer, and printer. Initially, I referred all my calls to the motel to avoid exorbitant cell phone bills. Then I discovered that none of the receptionists at the motel spoke English. Thank God for my friend Peter Bloch, who went into my home wearing a respirator to copy my hard drive and gather the relevant paperwork. And then I lost the hotel conference room that I had reserved; the check hadn't arrived on time. Still, I kept affirming that the workshop would be a success with the perfect people in the perfect place. The next day, a friend with a large home offered to host the workshop. This change of venue brought an unexpected boon—a group of employees from a company nearby decided to join us. Once again, I was shown that the best-laid plans sometimes are best laid aside.

The willingness to stay in my fertile soul followed me right up to the beginning of the workshop. Because I was still wardrobe-impaired due to my sudden move, I had rushed into a retail store to purchase a new suit on my way to the workshop. When my hostess introduced me, I stepped to the front of the room and looked down to see what was bumping my ankle. There I stood, in front of forty people, with a plastic security tag fastened to my pant leg! I looked upward, thanked God, and laughed out loud. At least the security guards hadn't detained me as I hurried out of the store. If you can hold all obstacles as part of your success, you can become a fertile soul.

I know the tools in this book work to enhance both access to your intuition and emotional adaptability because when I was guided in the dreamtime in late 2018 to leave California because disasters were coming, I followed that guidance to Asheville, North Carolina. I arrived one month before the fires occurred simultaneously in northern and southern California. I was warned in another dream that there would be more catastrophes in 2020 but I would be protected in Asheville. During the pandemic that began that very year, Asheville remained relatively well protected.

Vocation Breakthrough as Body Breaks Down

Who would imagine that their mission in this life could come from a disabling terminal illness? Although illness can certainly be a catalyst for leaving one life behind to begin another in stage four, it can also be the catalyst that solidifies the nature of your mission in stage six. For some people, their mission and their evolution in consciousness will actually require irrevocable breakdown in the body to fulfill their destiny.

The late Stephen Hawking was a bad student and a dilettante before he contracted ALS, an incurable degenerative disease. But that didn't stop him from becoming the rock star of quantum physicists. In *A Brief History of Time,* a documentary film about his life, Hawking acknowledges that the paralyzing nature of his illness helped him get focused.

Actor Michael J. Fox is another example of a man whose illness, in his case, Parkinson's disease, led to his life mission. The Michael J. Fox Foundation has raised over seventy million dollars for medical research. Not only did Parkinson's give Michael a higher purpose, but it also fundamentally changed him as a man. In numerous interviews, he's said that he has far more self-respect and is grateful for what his illness has given him.

Stage six is an inside job. You can have a fertile soul, no matter your circumstances. While rebuilding my immune system after toxic mold exposure, I had to cut back on public speaking. So I started doing radio and podcast interviews, and eventually telesummits and webinars, which gave me a new avenue to reach the whole world. If I was having a low-energy day, I could go on air without even getting out of my pajamas! The transition from stage five to stage six doesn't depend on having finally achieved a perfect life. What it does mean is that your mind has become agile enough to see the blessing in whatever the day delivers.

Healthy Wealth Practices

Another key to prosperity involves looking at your life as a bank account. As you receive healthy food into your body on a consistent basis, get enough sleep to regenerate the next day, and practice a form of exercise that is restorative, you make deposits into your physical bank account. As this becomes the nature of your daily life, the neuron pathways in your brain are balanced, enabling you to more effectively hold thought patterns that magnetize an abundant life. I cannot say enough about meditation or guided exercises to support these new grooves.

However, if you lapse into draining your bank account, you know you're in stage six if you bounce back quickly. It is very much akin to a former athlete's going through a phase where he stops working out and gains a lot of weight. When he decides to get back into shape, there is muscle memory to which the body responds. The mind and the emotional body work in a similar way. If you've done the work of the first five stages, your mind has become more agile. Therefore, even if you have a week where you regress into bad habits and toxic thoughts, you can snap back more easily by doing certain exercises.

During my recovery period, I began a practice of opening my crown to white light every morning. I specifically directed healing light into the system of my body that most needed it. If I woke up fatigued, I would put my hands on my mid-back and direct healing energy into my adrenal glands, which sit on top of the kidneys. (Much better for your adrenals than caffeine, don't you think?) Since my immune system was a weak link in my health, I would also direct the emotion of joy and healing energy toward my white blood cells, the intention being that they were getting stronger and stronger. I would thank them for doing such a good job of taking care of me. This practice is drawn from Dr. David Bresler's pioneering work at UCLA. Using guided visualization with cancer patients, Bresler has made a huge contribution to the field of mind/body medicine over the past thirty years.

If you find that you still have a chronic or terminal illness in spite of maintaining a fertile soul, you can still live a life of purpose. All the healers I've ever worked with maintain that healing is not synonymous with curing. Illness itself can be a teacher; your soul has a purpose for everything. Death is part of life, after all, and for many people the reality of death flips a switch in awareness that allows their remaining days to be filled with new meaning and insight.

Allow your body to speak to you through your illness. Talk with it. Ask the illness, "What are you here to teach me?" There is wealth there—a gift that may heal your soul, even if it doesn't cure your illness. In my next book, I will be taking a deeper dive into the power of *health-quakes* to transform your life.

Wealthy Relationships

The first four stages of *The LifeQuake Repurposing Roadmap* will change the way you relate to others. If you've relied on false structures, such as approval or substances to feel secure, your LifeQuake may have dismantled that shaky foundation. By stage six, your new relationships will begin to show signs of interdependence, and collaboration, which means depending on your own approval and yet staying connected to others. The key to wealth consciousness in your relationships is to tell the truth—all the time. When you believe that everything you need, will always be there, you come from the truth. And by truth, I mean listening to your intuition through intentionally merging your awareness into the Wholy Self. What does your intuition tell you to say and do with your spouse, your children, your mother, your friend, etc?

The other key ingredient to effective communication with others is to run it through your heart. For example, you need to tell a friend that the project he wants you to become involved with is something your gut is telling you isn't going to work. If you go into your heart and draw out your fertile soul to speak your truth, you can say no to someone and still remain connected. Most people hate to say no, so they close down their heart to get the word out. An assertive or aggressive energy colors their self-expression. Speaking from the heart will help you avoid adding unnecessary anger to your no.

When we tell the truth with kind strength that acknowledges our common vulnerability, no one experiences lack, even if one of the parties says no. One very important key to having a prosperous life lies in surrounding yourself with people who joyfully support your path. One of the many beautiful messages that Chellie Campbell conveys in *The*

Wealthy Spirit is to get rid of the sharks and cultivate dolphins as your friends and community.

In the words of Auntie Mame from the Broadway play *Mame*, "Life is a banquet and most poor suckers are starving to death." Many opportunities will come to you at this stage of consciousness. How do you choose which to take? For Luciano Copete, the key is to rely on other senses. He explains, "Close your eyes. Put your hands out in front of you and feel through your fingers the energy of which opportunities are for you. Does it feel warm like the light of the sun? If the world goes through major catastrophe in the coming years, we need to experience abundance in a new way, not how it looks. Practice this by paying attention to your ears, your tongue, and your hands. Listen to the beauty of animals singing, really taste the food you eat at every meal, and hug each other. Gauge the degree of your wealth by this."

If you truly are feasting at the banquet of life, your way of dealing with everyone will be generous. Kindness and compassion, mixed with the truth, makes for the wealthiest of relationships. Ultimately, people will trust you, and trust is what makes real intimacy possible.

Spiritual Tithing

Most books on prosperity consciousness highly recommend giving 10 percent of your earnings to charity. For anyone who is interested in understanding the principles of financial tithing in greater depth, I recommend reading *The Richest Man in Babylon* by George Clason. For our purposes here, I will talk about tithing only as it applies to energy.

Part of experiencing yourself as wealthy in this stage is to give 10 percent of your waking life in selfless service. You might say, "But I already do! I have children and a spouse, and they require much more than 10 percent of my time." What I want you to consider is another form of giving, one you can engage in with little things that happen all day long. For example, you let the woman who's in a hurry go ahead of you in the grocery line, or you direct a field of love around the guy who cuts you off on the freeway. You do these things, even if the woman has more items in her basket than you do, or if the guy scowls at you when he takes over your lane. Doing this makes a very important statement to your own psyche: "I have an abundance of time. I have all the time I need," or "If he's in that big of a hurry, he must need some loving energy." By not matching his energy, you might even de-escalate the man's negativity before he causes an accident. This type of spiritual tithing changes the way we experience strangers; this is a bridge practice to stage seven.

How can we experience ourselves as part of a global family (that includes countries who hate us) unless we can do that with difficult people? Begin each morning with a prayer to extend grace wherever it is needed. This is not about moral obligation. Extend grace to difficult people. Again, it's a paradox. All day long, the universe serves up opportunities to feel unjustly treated or to be a leader in transforming injustice.

Further, the development of the fertile soul that leads to global *humane-itarianism* in stage 7 requires a deep inquiry into the foundation of poverty both in yourself and in the world. In her book, *The Soul of Money*, Lynn Twist suggests that we examine what we spend money on as a reflection of the statements, "I am enough. I have enough." Is what you spend money on in alignment with the inner state of true wealth for you? Returning to one's bank account idea, Lynn suggests looking at your real bank and credit card statements and they will show you what you truly value in the world and yourself. We will learn more about Lynn's global work with her husband Bill Twist and *The Pachamama Alliance* in chapter seven.

Building Elements

The building elements in stage six are *gratitude, enthusiasm, and joy.* The word enthusiasm comes from the Greek word *entheos*—to be filled with God. When you're in a state of radiant light, you only attract work and intimate relationships that support the kind of enthusiasm and joy that is aligned with your highest destiny. If everything that happens to you is seen as grace, then gratitude comes as a natural extension.

Praying by the Numbers

Science agrees that the universe is vibration. The hypothesis of sacred geometry is that vibration is manifested on the visual time/space planes. The theory behind this particular discipline is that the universe is created by thought, which manifests in physical reality through a geometric blueprint. This view posits that we live in a mathematical universe that repeats in cycles. Plato said: "God geometrizes continually". In modern times, the mathematician Carl Friedrich Gauss adapted this quote, saying "God arithmetizes".

These scientific roots can be seen in the principles of sacred geometry, which was practiced by the Ancient Egyptians, Greeks, Romans, and Indians, and used in their architecture. We find numerous references in the Bible and of course, the Kabbalah. It is found throughout nature. For example, honeybees construct hexagonal cells to hold their honey. The exercise that follows can assist you in creating a sturdy container for your own 'honey' and will hasten your move into stage-six consciousness.

The practice of repeating certain numbers with a high intention and the emotion of joy changes your thoughts, and therefore, your overall consciousness. Just as quantum physics is theoretical, so is sacred geometry. What we do see empirically is that as our thoughts change, we attract abundance in accordance with our intention; this is the universal law of attraction. The mystery, however, lies in timing. The soul has its own timing as to how this vibrational change in our thoughts actually lands visibly in our lives. The study of the interaction between the planets in our galaxy and our soul blueprint is also mathematical in its evaluation of timing as to when things can happen. It is why I became an astrologer 25 years ago. I saw its efficacy, over and over and have found the study of sacred geometry and astrology helpful in supporting my clients in their careers, as well as to when to take action for the greatest desired results. Gregg Braden, author of *The God Code*, *The Divine Matrix,* and *The Science of Self Empowerment* as well as many other scientists have written on quantum healing and have shared volumes on how the universe is coded mathematically and moves in predictable cycles. He calls it the Divine Matrix.

I'd been meditating on a sequence of numbers that was given to me in a sacred geometry class about a year before my black mold exodus. One day, I saw a new sequence of numbers while meditating with my eyes closed. They came to me shortly after I started crashing again and spent days at a time in bed in the very room (unbeknownst to me) that contained the highest levels of mold in the walls.

Stuck in stage five, I was told that these two new sequences were to be used to accelerate the vibratory rate of my electromagnetic field and help my body to evolve. I have no way of proving it, but I believe that repeatedly affirming these master numbers protected me from permanent damage to my body from the invisible toxins in my house. Not only did I heal from a life-threatening illness, but everything I needed to re-create my life appeared at an even more abundant level than what I left behind.

Use this practice every morning and throughout the day whenever you need assistance in attaining overall wealth consciousness, perceiving the grace of any crisis or breakdown that comes in. You can also use it when you wish to accelerate your vibration into a joy-filled state and manifest specific intentions.

The Toolbox

Charging Your Batteries Visualization

Sit up with your back supported and take a few deep breaths into your belly. Chant out loud, making the sound "Om-m-m-m" as you exhale. Repeat the breathing exercise with "Om" seven times. Once you feel centered in your body, think of a moment in your past that brought you joy or made you laugh. Maybe it was something a pet did or a favorite childhood memory of yours. Where are you feeling that delight in your body?

Call in radiant light through the top of your head, and with joyful intention, affirm this statement out loud three times: "I now vibrate to the frequency of 11, 33, 44. I choose to experience gratitude, enthusiasm, and joy and claim success in all my experiences throughout the day." As you repeat the numbers, focus your awareness on something you want to have manifest in your personality or outer life. Inject your vision in the here and now with passion, and then release it, expressing your gratitude for whatever shows up.

The number eleven is considered a master number in sacred geometry. It represents light, electricity. The number thirty-three is also a master number in sacred geometry, the number of global service and unconditional love. The number forty-four represents inner and outer balance in one's foundation; it brings the highest order of manifestation. This exercise helps solidify the new structure of your life while preparing you for stage seven. Even if you don't believe that words or numbers have a mathematical frequency, if your intention behind the repetition is for joyful manifestation, you'll attract that reality to you.

For example, I did this exercise when my car broke down one morning. With fumes spilling out, I used the breathing technique from stage one for immediate fear-reaction to expensive car repairs. As I repeated the sacred numbers, I visualized something wonderful coming out of this experience, and it did. I left the garage feeling profound gratitude at how lucky I'd been that it was just a cracked hose instead of something more serious and how fortunate I was that I hadn't been in an accident over it. Developing the fertile soul of wealth consciousness is a heart to head game. We can come out of any experience and choose to see ourselves as prospering.

Developmental Steps to Change Mastery

✓ Expand your concept of wealth. Make lifestyle choices that authentically support your bountiful, inner bank balance and heart centeredness.

✓ Manifest tangible prosperity through transforming the perception of loss into gain from everything.

✓ Create miracles from a perception of appreciation and gratitude.

✓ Practice tools such as sacred geometry that structurally change your vibration and feeling tone into joy.

7

Everybody Wins: The New Game

Humankind has not woven the web of life. We are but one thread within it. Whatever we do to the web, we do to ourselves.

~ Chief Seattle

Onset

Through quantum physics and clinical studies, we know that through the act of observing something, not only is the observer changed but what is observed is changed as well. In stage six, we applied this concept internally. Through leaning back and observing our thoughts, rather than identifying with them, we can change our thoughts, and in so doing, we change as well. Every time we upgrade our thoughts, the vibration we emit changes and we contribute to a collective, paradigm shift in everyone.

By changing your thoughts about yourself and the world, the world itself will change.

While writing the first draft of this chapter, 11 years ago, the editor with whom I was working at the time challenged this idea and suggested I drop stage seven altogether. He reasoned that people don't really care about changing the world and that most just want to improve their own lives. I contemplated this and asked myself, "Who am I to write about unity consciousness?" My own experience of oneness with others comes and goes. I'm still subject to prejudices and conditioned states of mind that keep me separate from the world more than I'd like. I probed further, asking myself whether I'd ever done anything for anybody without an ulterior motive. And then I remembered something one of my grad school professors said many years earlier: "There is no such thing as a purely altruistic motive." And so began this leg of my journey and an exploration of a peculiar paradox: behaving altruistically seems to benefit me as much, if not more so, than those I serve. It just feels good to help others.

Now what has become so vitally important for everyone to know is that in this time when we have lost 50% of sea life in the past 40 years, changing our thoughts is critical to the mass consciousness shift it will take for us to reverse the climate crisis. Historically, we have lived in a paradigm of success based on competition and Darwin's theory of survival of the fittest. We must move into a consciousness of collaboration and cooperation for our collective survival and thriving.

Embracing the Paradox of Altruism

Once upon a time, there were triplets named Al, True, and Ism. Born to a mother who believed her sons were extra-special, she raised them to believe they each had a great destiny.

A child in the sixties, the triplets' mother wanted her children's names to invoke activism. Al was named for the abbreviation of his mother's birthplace and a famous city in the birth of the civil rights movement. She named her middle child for her favorite word, vowing to raise all three of her sons according to her core value—be true to yourself. And Ism, the youngest, was an abbreviation for the kind of action she respected most: heroism. She wanted her sons to be reminded how important courage was moment to moment. But most important, when she called their names, one after the other, she wanted to subliminally reinforce the message that when they grew up they would make a difference in the world.

On the boys' thirtieth birthday, their mother gave each son five thousand dollars and instructed them to take the money out into the world and help at least one person with it. Al took his five thousand dollars and helped a homeless guy get himself cleaned up, get an apartment, and get a job. True gave his money to a homeless shelter, with the stipulation that the money be spent directly on food—two thousand people received hot meals that week. Ism, being the most technology-savvy of the three, decided to do some research on the Internet. He learned about an approach to humanitarian aid that had become popular: micro-lending. He liked the idea that his money would actually help people get off the streets and out of shelters, permanently. He gave his five thousand dollars to a venture philanthropist firm that teaches people how to make inexpensive ceramic vases, loans them the money for the materials at a small interest rate, and helps them start a small cottage business. His five thousand dollars helped numerous families in the third world become economically independent. Now, which of these brothers is the wisest altruist? The answer is … all of them. Why? Each was following his unique purpose and making a difference with a mere $5000.

To achieve the final stage of your LifeQuake, you must align with your true purpose and become your version of an agent of change in the world, in order to fulfill your full potential. By now, you've gained some mastery of personal change, you've clarified your mission and purpose, and you've discovered the power and joy of giving service. You're ready to play a vital part in a conscious leap in human evolution. And the springboard that enables you to participate in this leap is the change mastery you gained by going through the first six stages of your Life-Quake. Now, in stage seven, you can become a change agent simply by using your soul's purpose and mission to change **your** world. Even if you focus on your local community and tribe, the change is happening exponentially.

Let's quickly review the territory we've covered so far. Would you agree that there is great benefit in learning to anticipate change, rather than waiting until a disaster hits? Would you agree that finding a graceful way to move into a new cycle of life warrants radical severance from the defunct one? And further, would you agree that designing a life that supports your fullest potential, is essential?

So what are the benefits of altruism? And how does it support your ability to master change? In a world where selfishness is consistently rewarded, why would anyone bother developing altruistic behavior?

Through the stories and suggestions of this stage, you'll discover that altruism not only makes the world a place where humanity can thrive, but it also makes you a happier person.

In chapter six, we worked with tools that helped you embrace the paradoxes of life in order to develop a fertile soul. When you master stage six, you're able to experience life's manure not as some toxic waste product that is poisoning you, but as fertilizer for a rich soil (the creative mind) that will produce abundant crops. The net effect of this is that you have less resistance and are able to more successfully manifest what you desire through the law of attraction. We build on this notion in stage seven. If you're hardwired toward self-survival, why would you act paradoxically in a manner that risks your survival for the sake of another?

Most sociological studies indicate that humans act altruistically most consistently to ensure group survival. During times of scarcity or conflict, we'll sacrifice our own well being to help ensure the survival of the group. This trait becomes self-perpetuating. The tribes whose mores were geared toward group altruism survived; therefore, this trait was reinforced. Those that were not became extinct.

When global LifeQuakes have manifested such as pandemics and Wall Street upheavals, people become kinder, extending themselves to help others. Case in point: when 9/11 hit, New Yorkers began exhibiting new behavior. There was more compassion and kindness, more willingness to help each other at a time when people were in a heightened state of shock and fear. When the ground of illusory security was pulled out from under them, New Yorkers banded together. Their very survival had been threatened, and their primal instincts to assist each other was activated. Hurricane Katrina brought people from all over the country to Lousiana to help. The same occurred in Haiti with the tusunami and now with social media, we banded together as a true global family to fight pandemics and climate change.

Gandhi stood alone against the tyranny of the British Empire, risking his life. Why? Perhaps his uniqueness stemmed from transcending his personal identity to embrace a larger self that encompassed his entire country, the people's suffering, and their need for liberation.

Teilhard de Chardin once said, "Union differentiates. When you become part of the whole is when you become fully yourself." Perhaps this is what we witnessed in Gandhi—he actually transcended self-survival into identifying with all the Indian people.

If that's the case, the question becomes: Was Gandhi a complete anomaly, or is it possible that now more than ever, the potential to identify with the whole human race is growing within all of us? As we evolve into stage-seven consciousness, might the expansion of a fertile soul extend beyond national identity into a planetary one? Further, just as our soul purpose needed to be uncovered in stage five, might we uncover an innate altruistic nature that is hardwired in those who are evolutionary human beings? Perhaps as we expand our sense of self to include everyone on the planet, the idea of altruism takes on a whole new meaning. No longer are we just nationalist altruists, helping our community when hit by disaster so the community becomes whole again. We are waking up to our responsibility to the entire human family. When we see ourselves as one tribe and one entity, we can no longer ignore what's happening to people on the other side of the globe. Assisting people in Africa or Southeast Asia affects us all; therefore, assisting them ensures our future survival.

Consider what happened with the AIDS epidemic. We mobilized aid when we discovered the virus had originated in Africa. That mobilization shone the light on Africa; other plights among the African people came to our attention as a result of that effort. Those already at stage seven, are now taking on these causes, such as solutions for creating clean water. They identified with the African people as part of one family. What is shared—our humanity—outweighs all differences, and science has now demonstrated this to be literally true.

Anthropologists have evidence that suggests that everyone in the world is connected to ancestry dating back 160,000 years to Africa. Sadly, it's our African relatives who need our help the most right now, as millions of people are **still** dying of AIDS and leaving millions of children orphaned. Globally, nearly 1000 girls and women ages 15 to 24 contract HIV every day, and the vast majority of them live in sub-Saharan Africa (the origin of many African Americans). Here, young women are twice as likely as young men to be living and dying of HIV. Perhaps those who devote their time to saving Africa really do understand that these people who share our ancestral history are family.

Not to minimize the pandemic begun in 2019, but globally, 32 million people have died of AIDS since that epidemic began and although it is possible with having access to the right drugs, one can live with it, it is also a deadly and serious chronic virus, not an acute one. Maybe there was a greater evolutionary mechanism at work in the AIDS epidemic that was the preliminary to global mobilization on other pandemics and climate change that are hitting us in this third decade: the lesson of oneness. What supposedly originated in Africa, became an epidemic here as well. What originated in Wuhan, China hit the U.S. the hardest but infiltrated almost every country around the world. Just as a personal LifeQuake humbles by dissolving the false boundaries of the ego so that we merge with the Wholy Self, our national identity is showing many cracks in its foundation, as a new identity of global citizenry appears on the horizon. The American Empire is over.

This is the gift of Global LifeQuakes. Humility and vision are crucial to breaking down barriers based on race, nationality or economics and igniting collaboration and cooperation.

We can anticipate change at this macro level, just as we can at the micro or personal level. We don't need to wait for a plague, terrorist attack, tsunami, or pandemic to compel us to work together. The current threats to our species' survival through climate change are real and sufficient to compel us to act now—and act swiftly.

"I Feel Good!"

The feeling of wellbeing that comes with doing for others is self-reinforcing, much like food and water. It just makes you feel good to help where you can, and your mind and body want more of that good feeling. Seen in this light, altruistic behavior is a totally different deed from the kind of self-sacrifice that comes from low self-esteem. In earlier chapters, we talked about the way addictions are transformed through *The LifeQuake Repurposing Roadmap*. The addiction transformed at this stage is co-dependency, the act of giving to others in order to feel needed or in order to receive something back. Inherent in the addiction of co-dependency is the belief in lack, the I-am-not-enough feeling that is linked with a belief that if I take care of you, you will be indebted to me. The "I feel good!" paradigm of stage seven makes the old motivations lose their luster. You do what you do because it feels good, pure and simple.

As part of the Wholy Self, who you are has expanded to include others, so that as you give, you simultaneously receive. You give from wholeness of self. If you want to geek out and understand this from the new physics, google "quantum entanglement theory." It gives us the hard science behind the concept that we all are a part of only one Self. Your journey through these seven stages takes you from initial dependency on the outer world for identity, to a relationship with your inner world that creates true selfhood, and finally to interdependence, in which you give and receive not just for survival but because it genuinely feels good.

I grew up Catholic and was taught that I should give until it hurts. How crazy is that? I call it the Martyrdom School of Humanitarianism. Unfortunately, pain doesn't evolve your soul in and of itself. Instead, it's joy that takes us into higher and higher states of consciousness. So use your inner wisdom to find the activities that bring you joy. All great beings that sacrificed themselves knew the real cosmic secret: states of ecstasy accompany true altruistic behavior because there is no resistance to discomfort.

The exercises and advice in this chapter are designed to energetically accelerate your evolution and promote genuine wellbeing. You'll hear from various visionaries and learn their techniques for evolving your higher potential. If you practice regularly, you'll experience yourself and all living things as part of the Wholy Self.

What is deep within our cellular memory is that we have fifty trillion cells in our body that are its own community and have its own economy. According to biologist Dr. Bruce Lipton author of *The Biology of Belief*, the body has its own bank so to speak. All the cells work together to keep the body in balance. If certain cells become deficient, they can withdraw energy (ATP) to rebalance. When your psyche goes into a belief system that you aren't enough or don't have enough resources, you deplete the bank too much and illness occurs. Further, he asserts that this is what is responsible for an outer reflection of a dis-eased planet.

In stage seven, one must understand that there is no separation between any of us; that what we do for others, we do *for* ourselves or *to* ourselves. In aboriginal tribes, this truth is known. All the more reason why protecting the natural world, is so important. These tribes understand and live in respect to each other and Mother Earth. We need their presence to make this shift ourselves. One of the last changes in identity that comes in stage seven is transcending nationality, race, and religion. From this perspective, altruism is actually a truly selfish act in the best sense of the word. Stage-seven mastery resolves the paradox of selfishness and selflessness; these co-exist as giving and receiving, merging in simultaneous pure joy.

Morphic Resonance

Descartes believed that the only kind of mind was the conscious mind. Then Freud discovered the unconscious. Then Jung identified the collective unconscious. Morphic resonance expands on that idea to show us that our very souls are connected with those of others and bound up with the world around us. "Morphic resonance is the concept of mysterious telepathy-like interconnections between organisms and of collective memories within species," declares Rupert Sheldrake, PhD. A former research Fellow of the Royal Society and a scholar of Clare College, Cambridge, and Harvard University, Sheldrake has been making waves in the world ever since his first book, *A New Science of Life*, burst on the scene in the 80's. The essential forces of morphic resonance are known as the morphogenetic field, a power that guides the development of an organism as it grows so that it follows in the footsteps of its predecessors. According to this theory, DNA is not the source of structure itself but rather a "receiver" that translates instructions from the field into physical form. Bruce Lipton has expanded on Sheldrake's work.

If Jung and Sheldrake are right, and we are connected by nonphysical means, it might explain why, for example, a mother just knows when her child is in danger—even if he is halfway across the world. If we take this a step farther and move outside of our family or tribe to people who create the same invention in two different parts of the world at approximately the same time, we might surmise that not only is it shared genetics that provides morphic resonance but shared consciousness. Some scientists refer to it as "nonlocal" consciousness.

After 9/11 occurred in 2001, I heard countless stories from people, both in New York and around the world, who all claimed that they experienced paranormal phenomenon in the days prior to the terrorist attack: people whose intuition told them not to take United Airlines, flight 93, people who had visions of planes attacking a building days before, or who (as was my experience) simply felt something catastrophic was about to happen. I thought a family member was about to die and spent all day on September 10 consumed by grief. I had the same experience in January of 2020, two months before we knew we were in a pandemic. I felt death around me so profoundly that I updated my will because I thought I might be the one about to die.

If a morphic resonance was formed by those who had a prescient knowing, isn't it possible for a morphic resonance to form amongst people who are altruistic, that will then expand exponentially in the quantum field? If Malcolm Gladwell is right, a tipping point of massive altruism could prevent catastrophe through practices that would shift our planetary future.

Survival of the Fittest or Who Fits Best

If we try to approach saving the world by taking on all the massive issues that catalyze planetary destruction, it becomes overwhelming. The average person becomes paralyzed just thinking about it, so we go into denial and pretend the problem isn't imminent.

Substantial evidence suggests that evolution occurs on multiple levels within a single species. Let's take human evolution as a case in point. It's been documented that Cro-Magnon man and Neanderthal man walked the earth at the same time. They co-existed in the Mediterranean area for at least 60,000 years. Many theories have been offered to explain the eventual extinction of Neanderthal man. What we know about Cro-Magnon man, is that he, unlike Neanderthal evolved the ability to form complex language.

Now, I'm postulating here, but what if the next leap in our evolution is the development of a normal human brain that could extend beyond one's immediate tribe to a natural planetary identity? It is theorized that the prefrontal "angel lobes" of the neo-cortex give one the capacity for altruistically seeing and responding to the needs of others. The practice that develops this is meditation. As more people are developing mindfulness practices, perhaps, it will spearhead the next leg of human evolution.

Bruce Lahn, an assistant professor of human genetics at the University of Chicago, has found through DNA analysis that there has been a recent evolutionary shift in the brains of some people. We're observing mutations that are expanding brain size. What if that brain expansion is somehow related to the growing development of the capacity for morphic resonance?

As scientists study the brain function of monks who spend a lot of time in meditation, they're finding very distinct and unique brainwave patterns. I believe we will find that the capacity of one to go deep into inner space also allows one to expand the consciousness of the mind to go far out into the collective consciousness of humankind. A practice of spending time in stillness not only builds inner peace, but it can be the most important thing we do to change the world. Even if you see the world as an unfriendly place, if you're willing to do something to change that perception and spend fifteen minutes a day envisioning yourself and the planet at its full potential, you will have done a great thing.

Heaven on Earth

Remember Martin Rutte from stages four and five? He's the visionary leader and business consultant who co-authored the book *Chicken Soup for the Soul at Work*. Martin's pioneering work on spirituality in the workplace was featured on the ABC-TV special *Creativity: Touching the Divine*, in which he addresses the World Bank. When I interviewed Martin about his latest book and mission Project Heaven on Earth: *the 3 simple questions that will help you change the world ... easily*, I asked if he'd ever intuited a catastrophe and acted in advance. He shared that at the end of 1993, he and his wife, Maida, were living in Sherman Oaks, California, in close proximity to the San Andreas fault. Within a two-week period they both "heard" an inner voice that said, "Get out by January 15." The synchronicity of this message was too great to ignore. They moved to Santa Fe, New Mexico, on January 14. The Northridge quake occurred three days later.

Once in Santa Fe, Martin began to go beyond his mission "to bring spirituality into business practices and the workplace, while reconnecting business with its natural source of creativity, innovation, and genius". He created Project Heaven on Earth, whose mission is: "to have heaven on earth be the new story of what it means to be human and what it means for us to be humanity."

In his seminars and speaking appearances, he asks three questions. Before reading the following sequence, get out a pen and your journal or a pad of paper. Take time to contemplate each question before you answer.

The Magic Wand Exercise

1. Tell me a time when you experienced Heaven on Earth.

2. Suppose you had a magic wand and could create anything you wanted for yourself, for others, for your work, for your community, for your nation, for the planet. And anything you created would be part of heaven on earth. Imagine you have this magic wand now. What would you create to help bring about Heaven on Earth? The power of the magic wand is that it relieves you of the necessity of knowing how something will be achieved, because that's the wand's job. Your only job is to be clear about what you want. Your job is to answer the question, "What do I want?" while the magic wand's job is to answer the question, "How will it be done?"

   Take a few moments now to use your magic wand. (You may want to pick up a pen or pencil and pretend it's the magic wand.)

3. What action steps can you take today that will help bring about what it is you want?

Martin elaborated: "Each person must define for [him/herself] what heaven on earth means. Just as it's important for you to get clear about your life purpose in order to live in alignment with what is authentic, it's also important to be clear as to what heaven on earth is for you. Most people don't even know such a concept can exist at such a time as this is on the planet, but when you ask them for a personal experience of heaven on earth, suddenly a space in their consciousness is created that makes it possible." For more information on this, go to **ProjectHeavenOnEarth.com**.

In keeping with Martin's project, start every single day by thinking of a time when you experienced heaven on earth. Then go to your vision of a global Heaven on Earth and make a commitment to doing something today that'll assist you in manifesting it. For example, if you're holding the vision for world peace, at the very least, make one gesture in your daily activities that transforms conflict into harmony. Finally, acknowledge yourself at the end of the day for your contribution to both yours and humanity's new story.

Martin Rutte's "The Magic Wand Exercise" is the first of many tools provided in this chapter that not only moves the world forward, but feels good doing it. None of us know when we will take our last breath on Earth. Perhaps the hereafter is informed by the state we are in when we die. If we never know when that will be, doesn't it behoove us to perceive our reality as heaven now, and then take action to make planet Earth a heavenly place to be?

Once again, to reiterate, because there is no such thing as linear time, there is a you existing in a parallel universe fully potentiated, who is already living an existence of heaven on earth undifferentiated from the full potential of others. When you visualize that reality with the feeling tone of what heaven on earth is for you, you can then collapse time and merge that self into your brain and heart and step into that full potential. Using terms from linear time, you are bringing a future you back through time into the present you.

The New La Famiglia

I grew up in a family that was composed of two distinctly different ethnic groups: the Italians and the Germans. What my mother and father had in common was a fierce loyalty to family. I spent every holiday throughout my childhood with a large assortment of extended family. Family, as a value is very close to my heart.

After the black-mold fiasco, I eventually moved into the only safe and relatively inexpensive neighborhood I could find on the west side of Los Angeles. Given my love of foreign cultures and a plethora of Jewish friends, I thought that moving into a Hasidic neighborhood would be fun. Most of my neighbors were Iranian Orthodox Jews. It was my first experience of being that close to—but definitely outside of—a tightly knit tribe. Excited at first, I was intrigued by their curly locks and intelligent eyes. But walking in the neighborhood turned out to be a very lonely experience. Not only would these Hasidic women ignore my greetings, they wouldn't even look at me. I felt shunned. This wasn't long after 9/11, and I found that my own prejudices reared their ugly heads, especially when I heard parents screaming at their children. After several attempts to speak rationally to people that hurled baseballs through our window at three in the morning, I decided the change would have to come from inside me. The next day, I went for a walk, having declared with utmost conviction that everyone I passed would be friendly. And by golly, it worked. It was nothing short of a miracle. Empowered by my experience on the street, I started sending loving energy to the family with six kids who lived in a two-bedroom apartment across from my house; the noise and screaming showed a definite improvement.

We can love the idea of a global family until we are tested in our own backyard. What are your prejudices? What keeps you from embracing all of humankind as part of your family? Observe your thoughts through the course of the day. How often do you generalize or stereotype people of different races? Pay attention to your beliefs and prejudices and then release them consciously into the Wholy Self.

I have often wondered if there's a higher force guiding seemingly difficult phenomena on our planet. I offer the following as a case in point. A tendency in the last 30 years has been to put off having a family until age late thirties and early forties, during which time infertility skyrocketed in the U.S. Meanwhile, on the other side of the globe, China instituted a one-child-per-family law in an effort to control population. The Chinese value boy children over girls, so suddenly, a huge number of female Chinese babies were up for adoption, and childless Americans joyously, gave these orphaned girls a home.

Celebrities have adopted children in third world countries and also assisted the villages these children came from. They have come under great criticism from some Americans because we have many orphans right here who need a good home. But what if all of this is part of a bigger evolutionary mandate to help us get outside the box of our nationalistic identity? By bringing Third World children here, maybe— just maybe—the planet gets smaller, and we become more able to experience the planetary family through these children and we can end xenophobia every time a global crisis occurs.

And then there are our own children. What are we doing to inspire altruistic behavior in our nuclear families or whatever children we come into contact with?

I was working with a client who complained about the amount of stuff that his family had collected that wasn't being used, so I suggested he take on a project with his four-year-old—they each would go through their belongings (for the four-year-old, this meant a whole lot of the toys that he no longer played with) and see what they could donate to needy families at Christmas. My client's initial response was skeptical, and he gave me a look that said "end of story." I suggested he simply ask his son to pick a toy he would like a child at the homeless shelter to have and simultaneously set an example by going through his own possessions, and take his son along to make the donations. When he did this, he was surprised to find that his son not only got on board but also wanted to meet the kids to whom he was giving his toys. Sometimes, we underestimate the natural generosity of children.

Noblesse Oblige

I learned the concept of noblesse oblige—"to those with more, more is expected" from my mother. She often took my siblings and me along when she took food to the shanty shacks on the south side of Phoenix. My brother Michael (a born entrepreneur) made a first try at business at the age of ten, when he installed a lemonade stand, in front of our house. It was a sizzling summer day in Arizona, and our house was on the corner of a very busy street. He came up with the idea to give 10 percent of his sales to the Muscular Dystrophy Foundation. Not only did he sell out, but, our daily newspaper, *The Arizona Republic* ran an article with his picture. Three years later, while working at his second job as a newspaper boy, Michael saved a local family by calling the police when he smelled smoke coming from their house. In his thirties, he went on to make millions as an entrepreneur. My mother instilled in us that success wasn't success unless you were also a humanitarian.

For Luciano Copete, whom we first met in stage three, the imprint of humanitarianism came from his father, a successful hotelier. "In spite of the fact that I lost my father at the age of ten, he was an important role model for me. He treated the workers in his hotels equal to his wealthiest customers, and I never forgot that. In spite of having great success as a creative director for some of the top companies around the world, my deepest satisfaction has come from helping non-profit organizations get their message out." In the ten years since LifeQuake was first published, Luciano and his company, Hexpose, has morphed, allowing him to be both an environmental artist and system analyst, merging humans with local environments and virtual networks, empowering the integration of art and science to increase our quality of life.

For more information on Luciano's work, go to **hexpose.com**.

The Workplace

Stage seven is a time to try some experiments in affecting people with your caring. Here's a favorite: While driving to work, send an intention of radiant light to your office building, then to your boss's office, then to all your co-workers and anyone else whose path you might cross that day. Notice if your day feels any different.

Regardless of whether you work from home or in a traditional workplace, before meetings, step back and notice where your mind is. Clear out everything before this now moment so that you can show up authentic and present without any residue from past challenges or conflicts. The aim is to clear out the energy of the last meeting or personal issues so as to allow your psyche to fully engage with co-workers or staff. Paraphrasing Eckhart Tolle, the essence of existing in fifth dimensional consciousness is to be fully present. You do not exist in the past or future.

Culture Clash

Even if you don't discriminate on the basis of skin color or nationality, you may have more subtle prejudices. Do you have a bias, positive or negative, toward people who are wealthy? How about toward those who have either more or less education than you? Do you make assumptions about people who've never married, are childless, or who've been married many times? Do you judge people on their spiritual or religious beliefs? What about a group of people whose beliefs, traditions, and lifestyle choices are the most different? Carl Jung once said, " Critical thinking is difficult. That's why most people just judge." What are ways that help you maintain a bigger perspective of humanity?

Mark Twain is quoted as saying, "Travel is fatal to prejudice, bigotry, and narrow-mindedness, and many of our people need it sorely on these accounts. Broad, wholesome, charitable views of men and things cannot be acquired by vegetating in one little corner of the earth all one's lifetime."

Traveling abroad expands one's perspective and view of the world in life-changing ways. For those whose budget doesn't allow for this, the Internet has provided a way through social media to make friends anywhere in the world. When a global crisis occurs and we can't travel, the opportunity to truly connect with your social media friends and develop a true planetary tribe has become possible.

Divine Coincidence

When you feel connected to the universe for support, you can adapt to any circumstance. You're spontaneous and alive, fully in the moment and ready for whatever comes down the pike. In earlier chapters, we talked about the role of divine coincidence in discovering your next soul purpose. We also looked at how it contributes to a resilient mind. In stage seven, divine coincidence also plays a part, allowing you to truly inhabit the moment and act on the inspiration to help others.

I hate to be late for appointments and am "directions challenged", so I left in plenty of time to make it to the talk I was scheduled to give at noon. I'd been asked to speak to a group of businessmen on the power of meditation to increase creative problem solving. Once I exited the freeway, I got lost (in spite of my maps app) and couldn't find the hotel. I stopped in a gas station, got directions, and prepared to drive away. As I waited for an opening in the traffic, I heard a tap at my window. A tiny elderly woman peered through my window and waved at me. I rolled down my window, and she explained that she'd missed her bus and would have to wait two hours for the next one that went to her neighborhood. She asked me if I would drive her home—her neighborhood, mind you, was twenty minutes in the opposite direction of my destination. I was already late, but I agreed to take her. She hopped in, and off we went.

Needless to say, I arrived very late for my seminar. I made my apologies and began my talk by telling the story of what had just happened. "I am a punctuality fanatic, you see. Had I not meditated this morning, I'd be a complete wreck right now and a bad example of creative problem solving." This introduction broke the ice in the best way imaginable, with laughter, and the whole room visibly relaxed.

I couldn't have planned a better opening for a group that I'd been warned would be quite skeptical. I believe my aged passenger was put in my path for just that reason. When you're fully present, you can quickly assess and address the needs of others, even in unexpected or extreme circumstances. Aligned with synchronicity, you can allow yourself to follow what inspires you, even if there's a risk involved. As you stretch your boundaries, you learn to be less concerned with the opinions of others and more willing to take risks that allow your real strengths to come forward.

If you've built a fertile soul in stage six, you can harvest the good from any situation. This makes it easier to see the potential for planetary harvest in the face of what appears to be scorched earth. Climate change becomes far more than a looming threat in this scenario; it's a catalyst for a conscious, evolutionary global shift.

Back in the early stages of your LifeQuake, the proactive stance you had to take when your personal life started to atrophy is just as important at this stage; changing the world also requires daily practice. We're most willing to continue repeating actions that produce a good feeling in our bodies. Visualizing a fully-realized planet not only produces a good feeling in your body, it perpetuates doing good in your daily life, which then also perpetuates a good feeling in your body. And so the ripples of consciousness can spread.

Inner Sanctuary as an Altruistic Act

Begin your day by making a declaration of generosity toward those with whom you'll interact with that day. You might even make a ritual of doing these three times a day, at the beginning of a meal. You needn't make an elaborate production of it; simply send positive energy toward those that come to mind. In this way, you increase the goodwill and literally add to the bioelectrical current of love and kindness wherever you go. Visualize your gestures or generous thoughts having an exponential effect. With your intention, you can join a vast movement, a whole group of people who share the same intention to move the world forward into its full potential.

Purposeful Partnership

Partnership at the seventh stage fulfills two mandates: 1) a support for your soul purpose, and 2) a commitment to that which is greater than you both. At this stage, a commitment to serving the world and serving your partnership(s) are one and the same. Loyalty and devotion to each other's higher purpose accelerates growth and transcendence of ego.

Carl Jung spoke at length on the importance of the sacred marriage—the wedding of the inner man and inner woman within an individual that makes a fully realized partnership with another possible. To give a window into this type of partnership, I interviewed two couples who have lived an evolutionary path of purpose filled partnership in different arrangements: Barbara Marx Hubbard and Sidney Lanier (both of whom have since passed since *The LifeQuake Phenomenon* was first published) and Lynne and Bill Twist, the ongoing founders of the The Pachamama Alliance.

I first met Barbara, one of the early pioneers of The Human Potential Movement. A mutual friend invited her to a dinner party at my home. Mesmerized by her eloquence, I was startled to hear her put words to a phenomenon I'd only just begun to experience— something she called conscious evolution. In the years since that initial meeting, Barbara became a friend and mentor. Although I know many couples in conscious partnership, I chose to interview Barbara and her partner, Sidney, in this chapter because they met late in life, and yet had an alternative type partnership. They embodied a new paradigm for co-creative, elder relationships, a most needed model as we move into this next level of our evolution.

Barbara and Sidney had both been married before, and each had been highly visible and influential in their careers. But let's back up and take a look at the traditional relationship dynamics they both had to transcend in order to forge their unique partnership. I included their story in depth because in spite of her coming of age story starting over 60 years ago, the women I work with who are educated and raising children, come to me today with the same struggles around discovering their purpose, while juggling family life.

Beginning in her childhood, Barbara felt a pull to live a life of meaning and purpose, and yet the cultural mandates of the 1950s gave her few options. She got married, had five children, and settled into family life in suburban Connecticut with her artist husband. Then, in 1962, she read Betty Friedan's book, *The Feminine Mystique*. At last, someone had articulated the source of her sadness and created a dignified context for her longing. Along with an entire generation of women, Barbara's desire for an identity beyond that of wife and mother could no longer be dismissed as neurotic. The Feminist Movement began in earnest and although her husband shared her interest in living a life of purpose, he preferred that she stay in the background as his editor. Barbara's own voice would not be stifled, however, and she wrote a letter to *The Scientific American*—a leading-edge magazine of the time expressing her early thinking on conscious evolution. Her letter came to the attention of Jonas Salk, the physician who developed the first polio vaccine, and the two began a correspondence. The friendship with Salk proved a turning point for Barbara. Her essential nature as a visionary had been recognized. "He saw behind the Connecticut housewife persona to who I really was," Barbara recalled.

Eventually, Barbara divorced and wrote her first book, *The Hunger of Eve: A Woman's Odyssey Toward the Future.* Her thoughts about the evolutionary importance of space travel were confirmed while watching John Glenn circle the earth and seeing Her from space. This was clearly the next step in our birthing process. By now, a woman with both a voice and authority as a futurist, Barbara concluded, "If we could see ourselves from a distance, we could gain a greater perspective of ourselves. Just as in meditation, when we travel through inner space we develop the observer self, when we were able to actually see the whole of our planet from a distance, so birthed the cosmic observer self. We truly are not our city, our state, or even our country. We are planetary citizens. This perspective most probably launched the environmental movement in the seventies."

Barbara spent several years alone, keeping company primarily with women for the first time in her life. Like Freidan before her, she became a spokeswoman and advocate for the emerging evolutionary feminine. She observed that "liberated women" often fell into the trap of modeling themselves after men and submerging their feminine instincts. Many women had begun feeling dissatisfied with their jobs and yet were unable to identify what was missing. Inside of every man and woman, she asserted, is a need to do work that expresses their creative potential.

When Sidney came into her life, Barbara knew she'd met a man who had a healthy balance of masculine and feminine energy. Having been raised by a single mother, Sidney was keenly aware of the unfairness that women encountered in the workplace. As an army officer, he was exposed to the hyper-masculine archetypes typical of the military. However, his inner feminine would not be repressed and was expressed through his love affair with Mother Church. He loved the celebration of sacred community that the Church provided and entered the Episcopal priesthood. In time, however, he became disenchanted with the limitations of religion and left the priesthood. He then formed the American Place Theatre Group in New York and started the first residential human-potential center in Spain, La Finca. Perhaps Sidney's creative embodiment of the new male is what inspired his cousin, the iconic author Tennessee Williams, to fictionalize him in the character of a defrocked bishop in his novel *The Night of the Iguana.*

By the time he met Barbara, Sidney was twice divorced with grown children. He described his first marriage as purely physical, his second as intellectual. His relationship with Barbara was of another order altogether, an initiation and journey into a partnership of four entities: a whole man and woman inside himself, and a whole woman and man inside of her. As two wholes, rather than "better halves," they formed a truly co-creative partnership.

Their journey included living together, breaking up, and then reconfiguring into a new form. They referred to themselves as "permanently engaged". One of the techniques they found useful when they couldn't hear each other comes from the psychologist Hal Stone (introduced in chapter four), who created a psychological approach for working with your sub-personalities, called voice dialogue. To use this tool in your relationship, I suggest reading Hal and Sidra Stone's book, *Embracing Each Other.*

Barbara and Sidney's willingness to work with each other's subconscious selves paid off. They eventually found a balance in which they work together some of the time. This led to the development of cofounding *The Foundation for Conscious Evolution,* which still exists today. For more information on any of these projects, you can go to **BarbaraMarxHubbard.com** where her legacy lives on.

The other couple I interviewed are Bill and Lynne Twist. Lynne is the author of *The Soul of Money* and one of Oprah's go to influencers. Lynne and Bill are an example of a couple who had lived a somewhat traditional marriage for many years but one that evolved in step with Lynne eventually taking the visible lead.

In the early days of their marriage, Lynne was a homemaker but when she took the EST (Erhard Seminars Training) training in the late 70's, she began to wake up to her own calling and voice. As a child, she adored her father and very much wanted his approval. At age 13, Lynne's father died and her mother became overwhelmed with the responsibility of supporting 4 children. Lynne became close to a Catholic nun and began her "secret life" away from her outer life of Homecoming Queen and football games.

She would visit a Catholic retreat center telling her friends she was going to visit her grandmother. At the time, as is so often with children trying to make sense of a parent's death, she believed she was responsible in some way for her father's death. Had she been a perfect child, he wouldn't have died. Although her reasoning was originally driven by Catholic guilt and magical thinking of repentance, it provided the exposure to this word *calling*.

Having seen *The Nun Story* with Audrey Hepburn, initially she thought of becoming a nun because that was what nuns did, they had a calling. Although it would be years later when Lynne took up her own calling, this early experience provided the seeds that eventually allowed Lynne to wake up. In every hero or heroine's journey, the hero usually loses a significant parent at a young age. Lynne losing her father at a young age may have initiated her into becoming a leader early on. Synchronistically perhaps, age 13 is often when many tribal and religious sects create ceremonies for stepping into adulthood.

She and Bill met at Stanford, married and assumed an upper middle class life as Bill was on the fast track in the business world and Lynne became a homemaker. During her experience with the EST training and Werner Erhardt, Lynne had her first awakening as an adult when she realized that the life they were living was devoid of true service. Later, Lynne got involved with The Hunger Project, an offspring of EST, where she met Buckminster Fuller and John Denver. After many adult years influenced by powerful men, the turning point in her path, came through Joan Holmes, the founding president of The Hunger Project. Lynne acknowledged Joan as being the single most important person who shaped her into the leader she is today and through whom it became possible to eventually become director of The Hunger Project at an international level. Lynne and Bill's lives took on a deeply significant spiritual tone through their involvement, as they stepped into a huge commitment to Buckminster Fuller's vision of "a world that works for everyone with no one left out."

Further, the belief that not enough food was the symptom, not the problem, she took on the bigger conversation of ending the deeper disease of people believing they don't have enough and are not enough. The solution comes from a commitment of transforming who we are as a species, where we orient toward what she calls *sufficiency*: each person having a core self foundation of first being enough and then believing you have enough, so that no one on the planet is left out. Much of the revelations and inspirations for her book *The Soul of Money* came from her experiences there and much of her thesis of sufficiency as part of ending world hunger was influenced by her experiences there.

What else happened through both Lynne and Bill's mutual experiences at The Hunger Project was an evolution of their relationship into a marriage that lives inside a bigger commitment. Although Bill had also taken the EST training and supported Lynn's work at The Hunger Project, their work together with The Pachamama Alliance did not come until they were called by a friend, John Perkins (*Secret History of the American Empire*) to come to Guatemala. Like so many people who are called to a mission, both Lynne and Bill had both reached a pinnacle in their work at The Hunger Project.

On this visit they were initiated through a shamanic ceremonial journey. They both had profound mystical experiences that opened each of them to hear the call of the indigenous tribes in Ecuador. This eventually led to partnering with the Ashwar people, an indigenous tribe in the Rain Forest of Ecuador, and creating a foundation with efforts to protect the Amazon from oil drilling. That foundation is called The Pachamama Alliance an organization that is dedicated to protecting our natural resources in the Amazon and the indigenous people worldwide. **pachamama.org**

As a divine coincidence would have it, this area contains some of the highest concentrations of biodiversity on the entire planet. It is an area of immense ecological significance.

What I experienced from my interview with Lynne and Bill Twist was that when you have a shared mission in your relationship and you stand for each other's purpose toward the world, mutual power and respect comes naturally. Lynne said it best, " We don't stand facing each other but side by side serving humanity's future."

As you can see through the lives of these pioneers, evolutionary partnership isn't just co-creative but co-evolutionary, in that the partnership is a mechanism in which the individual comes to express his or her fullest potential through the relationship, while living inside a bigger vision.

Further, even for those not in romantic partnerships, every person you spend time with is a potential partner and collaborator. If you volunteer or give to a charitable organization, you are partnering.

The Transfunctional Body

By stage seven you've been given a multitude of health practices that strengthen your body's immune response and help you evolve your body, mind, and spirit into an organism that can foresee and adapt to change quickly and resiliently. In this chapter, we'll explore techniques that enhance health through being a "humane-itarian"—one who not only is devoted to the betterment of humankind but recognizes no difference between being the helper and the helpee. The aim of all health practices in this stage is to feel good and enhance your experience of now identifying with the oneness of all life.

When I began doing research for this chapter, I asked myself this question:

Are the "humane–itarians" the ones who are going to evolve and thus, survive this next step? Given that we're investigating evolutionary change, is there any support for the idea that altruism makes you healthier? Dare I suggest that evolution selects for altruists, that it is these individuals and their genetic makeup that might be required for the continuation of our species?

According to Joshua Morganstein, MD, chair of the American Psychiatric Association Committee on the Psychiatric Dimensions of Disasters, "selfless actions during a pandemic or disaster can be a key to recovering from one's own trauma. Altruism is one of the most powerful tools against negative thinking and inward focus."

Further, numerous studies have looked at people who volunteer their time and compared them to a control group who didn't; they have found that T-cell count actually increased in those who volunteered. This was further shown to be present in a very specific group of long-term HIV/AIDS survivors. Many of them were found to have become involved in some kind of volunteer activity.

A few years ago, the ABC News show *20/20* aired an interview by John Stossel with Stephen Post, PhD, author of *Why Good Things Happen to Good People*. Post has continued to write extensively on his research into the effects of altruism on depression and health. He conducted a clinical trial that used a self-report questionnaire at the beginning and end of the study. He asked a group of college students, who had no experience doing volunteer work before the study, "What percent of the time are you calm, centered, and relaxed?" The choices were one of four, ranging between 25 percent and 100 percent. At the onset of the study, the average response was 25 percent of the time. Subjects were then sent off to volunteer at a charitable organization. They were given the same questionnaire again three months later. This time, on average, the students reported feeling calm, centered, and relaxed 75 percent of the time.

These studies indicate that altruism has beneficial effects on the body, when practiced as a balanced extension of one's energy. However, there are ways to be a humane-itarian, other than volunteering your time. Every morning, before you get out of bed, either visualize or feel a radiant light filling your body, just like in previous chapters. Now, in stage seven, you'll extend that light to the whole world. Set an intention for seeing or feeling the world as a healthy place to live. Additionally, hold an intention that humanity will collectively shift its consciousness and begin to generate solutions to planetary issues, from social justice to global warming. Imagine a world where we have naturally selected for population control, thus eliminating the need for plagues and disasters that reduce the population. See our world populated by healthy men, women, and children. Feel the possibility of wellbeing in your body, and allow that to radiate across the world.

So what do you do on those days when you wake up, and you just don't feel optimistic or generous toward the world? What if fatalism takes over, and you just can't see past the thoughts that say we aren't going to survive this crisis du jour of the moment? First of all, find the feelings of despair or negativity in your body, just as you learned to do in chapter four. Breathe into those areas by placing your hands on the part of your body where you experience the feeling; then fill it with the light coming down through the top of your head and set an intention for healing.

Imagine that you're a diamond with carbon spots covering it. Allow the light to exert enough pressure to transmute the carbon so that its real essence can come through. If you feel an emotional shift, then begin expressing your gratitude for at least three blessings in your life. If you don't have a shift, go back to a memory from the past where you were very happy. Experience that feeling deeply and fully. Now let your whole body fill with joy from that memory; then bring in an inventory of things you are genuinely grateful for.

If affirmations work for you, the following four can really set your day. Say them slowly three times, with your hands over your heart while you are just waking up.

I am at peace with myself.
I am at peace with my body.
I am at peace with the world.
The world is at peace.

Finish with a prayer or by sending good intentions to the people in your life and holding them in radiant light.

How do you feel? If your energy has shifted, program yourself for the day ahead and see yourself extending this joy and gratitude to everyone you meet.

Our immune system is directly affected by how much power we feel to exact a change in our mood, as well as in our ability to make a difference in other people's lives. You cannot simultaneously enjoy giving to others and feel miserable. One feeling has to dissolve for the other to take hold.

Another health practice that is vibratory in nature is talking to the water you drink and/or the food you eat. Japanese researcher Masaru Emoto wrote the book *Messages from Water*, in which he asserted that human vibrational energy, through thoughts and emotions, can affect the molecular structure of water. Until his death, Mr. Emoto had been visually documenting these molecular changes in water by means of his photographic techniques. He froze droplets of water and then examined them under a dark-field microscope that has photographic capabilities. His work clearly demonstrates the diversity of the molecular structure of water and the effect of the environment upon the structure of the water. His research indicates that a toxic emotional environment will produce toxic water, whereas a pristine environment produces healthy water.

If you consider that we are 70% water, how we talk to ourselves makes us toxic or healthy. I would venture to say that putting our hands above our food and beverages and then sending an intention of love and healing can make quite a difference in the vibrational frequency of the meal.

Accelerating the Body's Stress Response

The immune system is challenged when we think and feel we are under threat. The sympathetic nervous system becomes activated when there is a crisis or emergency. This shuts down the parasympathetic nervous system that governs the normal functioning of the autonomic nervous system, which controls digestion, respiration, blood pressure, etc. The sympathetic nervous system gets our adrenaline going; it evolved to help us escape predators in prehistoric times. What's happened in contemporary times is that the sympathetic nervous system is on too much of the time. We are constantly under stress, and the unconscious has become programmed to experience that stress as chronic emergency. Research now shows that most diseases are created by stress. Therefore, if you learn to manage your stress, your body has the capacity to heal itself.

Most of our stress is unconscious, however, so healing has to take place on a quantum level. The body responds to energy generated by the mind and the emotions emitted from thoughts. Therefore, healing the body and overall health at stage seven occurs through the power of the mind, to align with a vision of radiant health that already exists in multi-dimensional reality. Again, we are in essence, collapsing time. When we've mastered stage six and can hold the paradox of diagnosed apparent disease with the declaration of radiant health, it's possible to reverse the pattern of reflexive unconscious stress and thus reverse the pattern of disease.

This bears repeating: evolution is not contingent on survival of the fittest but survival of what fits best for mother earth and humanity's thriving. In all our previous stages of evolutionary development, we needed fear to get our adrenaline pumping and move us away from predators. The species we're evolving into needs to eliminate constant fear and the overuse of the sympathetic nervous system for it to "fit best" in a world that is rapidly changing. How can we possibly adapt if our minds resist the continual modifications that are demanded?

Every time your phone, computer, or entertainment device is upgraded, you will grit your teeth and react. If you multiply that times all the other changes demanded in the workplace, your body is going to be marinating in irritation and annoyance. And those are just the day-to-day triggers. What about the impact of massive earth changes, increasing environmental toxicity, or the disintegration of society as we have known it? Given all of these conditions, it becomes essential to develop the ability to establish a state of calm, in spite of it all.

Ben Johnson, MD, DO, ND, whom you first met in chapter one (you might remember him from the book and DVD *The Secret* and author of *The Secret of Health: Breast Wisdom*), shared with me a spiritual technology that has the potential to shut off the sympathetic nervous system when we're not under physical threat.

As mentioned in chapter one, Dr. Johnson's first LifeQuake involved a serious spinal injury that led him to study alternative medicine and open a cancer clinic in Atlanta, Georgia. But a successful practice in alternative healing didn't cure his type-A behavior; the stress of success meant he was essentially unable to relax. In 2002, he began having involuntary muscle contractions in his legs. After a year of ignoring the symptoms, he sought the advice of an orthopedic surgeon, who diagnosed him with ALS—amyotrophic lateral sclerosis, often referred to as Lou Gehrig's disease. This progressive neurodegenerative disease affects nerve cells in the brain and the spinal cord. Motor neurons reach from the brain to the spinal cord, and from the spinal cord to the muscles throughout the body. The progressive degeneration of the motor neurons in ALS patients eventually leads to death. Dr. Johnson got a second opinion that offered the same diagnosis; he was told that he had about eighteen months to live.

Having dealt with ALS patients in his clinic, he knew that alternative medicine had little to offer. He tried electro-dermal screening and other energy medicine technologies to no avail. Then he met Dr. Alex Loyd, who taught him a spiritual technology that became a manual called *The Healing Codes*.

Within six weeks, Dr. Johnson's symptoms disappeared, and soon thereafter, his neurologist confirmed that the ALS appeared to be gone. Dr. Loyd and Dr. Johnson subsequently joined forces and were conducting healing seminars across the country since 2004 until Dr. Johnson's sudden death in 2019. Perhaps he has joined Wayne Dyer, Barbara Marx Hubbard, and Louise Hay whom I am told are working with humanity from the other side.

I included this healing technology at stage seven because this form of energy healing places special emphasis on giving and receiving. People are instructed to use the codes at home and reciprocate healing sessions with family members. Dr. Loyd observed that healing one's physical, emotional, and spiritual bodies results in people becoming more generous in other parts of their lives. When ordinary people are able to use their own hands to channel healing energy, rather than depending on a health practitioner, they get a direct experience of the unified field between giver and receiver. "No one is the guru or healer in this work," reported Dr. Johnson. "It comes through an exchange of love." For more information, contact Dr. Johnson's former partner and the pioneer of *The Healing Codes*, Dr. Alex Loyd. His book and program of the same name can be found at **thehealingcodes.com**

Building Element

Quantum altruism is the building element of stage-seven consciousness. Our genetic cousin, the chimpanzee, instinctively knows that altruistic behavior toward his fellow chimps ensures his survival, and thus, the survival of his species. We must expand this instinctive trait for survival. In stage seven, we transcend tribal consciousness and leave the ape-clan mentality behind. Even a nationalistic identity is too small for us at this stage. Our worldwide family is calling out to us to join them and leave no one out.

The Toolbox

Life Review

This final exercise for stage seven is meant to connect you to your entire life path. Most spiritual philosophies have some version of Judgment Day, some way of conducting a life review. "Die, but don't perish," says the Tao, and nothing drives home the truth of this quite like a Life-Quake. You learn to die while you're alive, many times over. In this way, over a lifetime, you shed your skin again and again, as old identities and ways of being are outgrown. A more authentic you emerges with each new cycle, as does a unique intelligence that lets you read the signs and consciously release what no longer fits with dignity—the same dignity some people evidence on their deathbed.

Set aside a few hours and review your journey since you began stage one of your LifeQuake. If you're reading this book straight through before you have mastered stage seven, review your LifeQuake as thoroughly as possible. Again, keep in mind that this is a quantum model where there is no real future linear time, and in that sense, you're already in your full potential self in a parallel universe version of you.

Write down the major events, people, places, and things that marked the way. Capture feelings that come back to you, snippets of conversation—write them all down. As you begin to understand both your soul purpose and the form it's taking through your mission, connect the dots with where you are now, as you read this chapter.

What are you giving energy to now? How do you fit into the planet's evolutionary future? To quote Mother Teresa, how are you operating as "God's pencil?" Acknowledge yourself for all the ways you are contributing to a global shift toward a more humane humanity. Further, write and describe who you would be if you were being an extraordinary person living an extraordinary life. Now, feel yourself as that person in every cell of your being.

Our journey to connect as one global family, one entity, began in stage one through our personal and collective LifeQuake. We began to awaken from a massive sedative, a drug that had us believing that our security and identity came from monetary values. As we unplugged from the matrix, the tremors began when that identity no longer gave us sustenance or stability. The boredom and ennui that appeared were the early glimpses of awakening to a deeper, soul-based identity. For some who were resistant to change, the material world was eventually ripped away. However, as the awakening of our soul's new life purpose emerges into conscious awareness, we're beginning to throw off inauthentic images and programs of ourselves, while seeking our true purpose and mission.

As we connect to something bigger than ourselves, this expansion of our psyche reconstructs into a form that is highly adaptable. If you knew that you could manifest whatever you needed through clearing unconscious beliefs and directing your thoughts, you'd be very detached from any job, relationship, or prized material object when it no longer served you. You could also detach from the media's take (part of the matrix) on the economy and know you can thrive by keeping your mind agile – able to see and seize opportunity daily. In this new paradigm, you can have great wealth in whatever form you desire it, without it having you. If you truly identify yourself with who you *really* are, you will know that everything is impermanent, and the soul is all you truly have anyway.

As you increasingly identify more and more of who you are as part of a greater whole, your boundaries of a separate self dissolve, and your intuition grows exponentially. As it deepens and expands, you're able to make changes on the spin of a head of a dime, and you really do become, as Jonas Salk phrased it, "part of a humanity that survives because it fits best with what the world needs to evolve".

To summarize, in stage seven we adapt to change with trust, knowing that everything we do for others and our planet Pachamama is a gift to ourselves. This hero's/heroine's journey and the collective *LifeQuake* journey, is an initiation that embodies not only psychological individuation but spiritual and physical individuation as well. Because this is a quantum model, you may feel yourself in some of these stages non-sequentially or even simultaneously. Even if you feel you haven't mastered the previous six stages, do the exercises in stage seven. There are more of them on my website. By the time you have mastered the tools of stage seven, your body, mind, and spirit will have passed through an evolutionary process. Your courageous, chaotic journey is exactly what is required for humanity to reach the tipping point that takes us into thriving on planet Earth.

The most amazing thing about participating in this evolutionary revolution is that there is no in-between. In the latter 4 decades of the 20ᵗʰ century, the assassination of four great leaders from politics, social activism, and music (John and Bobby Kennedy, Martin Luther King, and John Lennon) gave us one important message for our future: it is up to us to be our own heroes. And it is living out of this decision that will move our planetary family into a conscious, evolutionary leap. It takes everyday heroism from each of us. It takes a commitment to find inner peace and kindness, then extend that to others. It takes a willingness to develop green practices that bring our Great Mother back into balance.

If you've read this book to the end, congratulations! You've made the leap. You've chosen to become a transfunctional being: you are mastering change by dropping into your subconscious mind through breathing into the body, clearing any fear-based emotions, and then accessing the super-conscious quantum field for solutions or answers. Your relationship with change will never be the same. You may not be masterful yet at anticipating the when, what, and where to take action, but you are learning the nature of cycles, understanding the illusion of fail-safe material security, and strengthening your brain's ability to take its marching orders from the heart, forming true coherence. You're now part of the shift. Remember, you're not alone. The entire world is shifting with you.

Developmental Steps to Change Mastery

✓ Change the way you see the world so the world is a Wholy Self: everything and everyone connected in their fullest potential.

✓ Replace the need to be special with actuating your unique soul purpose.

✓ Directly address your daily conflicts, knowing its effects on the fate of world peace.

✓ Receive joy from serving others.

Notes on Chapter Seven

1. *Adventures in the Bone Trade: The Race to Discover Human Ancestors in Ethiopia's Afar Depression.* Jon E. Kalb. Published by Springer, 2001

This book chronicles the exploration of this unique desert area, focusing especially on the 1970s, when the valley was mapped and many fossils and archeological sites were discovered. The author gives his personal account of the twenty-five years he spent researching the region. As cofounder of the team that discovered Lucy, Jon Kalb has firsthand knowledge of the research that was involved in the findings of this region and of the intense rivalry that has accompanied those findings.

2. This idea of the transcendent brain (angel lobes in the neocortex) came out of neurologist Paul MacLean's work, *The Evolutionary Neuroethology of Paul MacLean: Convergences and Frontiers*, Praeger Publishers, 2003.

3. "America, the Charitable: A Few Surprises"
   Reported and written by Mark Trumbull for the *Christian Science Monitor.* Nov. 27, 2006.

The urge to make a difference and to take satisfaction in it outweighs monetary considerations. For example, a survey of 945 ultra rich individuals by Bank of America and the Center on Philanthropy at Indiana University found that slightly more than half would give the same amount, regardless of whether the estate tax or deductions for charitable giving were repealed.

None of this means that tax policy is trivial for charitable giving.

But the survey suggests that Americans' penchant for giving isn't driven primarily by tax breaks.

4. "Interactive model of women's stressors, personality traits and health problems." Janet W. Kenney, RN, PhD, & Anu
Bhattacharjee, MS, *Journal of Advanced Nursing,* Dec. 25, 2001.

Women with medium or high stressors and low assertiveness, low hardiness, or the inability to express their feelings were more likely to report physical symptoms than women who were stronger in these personality traits. Also, women with medium or high stressors and low to medium trusting or love relationships were very likely to report high emotional symptoms, as much as were women with high trust or love, who did not express their feelings. Assertiveness seems to be a key to a strong immune system.

5. *Research on Altruism and Love: An Annotated Bibliography of Major Studies in Psychology, Sociology, Evolutionary Biology, and Theology*

Byron Johnson, Stephen Garrard Post, Michael McCullough, Jeffrey Schloss. Templeton Foundation Press, 2003

6. Dr. J. Andrew Armour, a leading neurocardiologist on HeartMath Institute's Scientific Advisory Board, has found that the heart contains cells that synthesize and release hormones such as epinephrine (adrenaline) and dopamine, among others. It was discovered that the heart also secretes oxytocin, commonly referred to as the "love" or "bonding" hormone. Remarkably, concentrations of oxytocin produced in the heart may be as high as those produced by the brain. When you are altruistic – lending a helping hand – your oxytocin level goes up, which helps relieve your stress. Altruistic behavior also may trigger the brain's reward circuitry – the feel-good chemicals such as dopamine and endorphins.

However, the hormonal benefits of the good deed depend on the genuine intent of the act of altruism.

www.heartmath.org/articles-of-the-heart/generous-others-youll-happy/?fbclid=IwAR2-T4QlD66d6C1rZ9lU-mnbi4vk0Byb4VhzAVmIM7FEPSVWbTfurLSZoqU

Epilogue

Imagine a life where you aren't afraid of major change, where you can intuit the ending of a cycle well in advance, while still preparing for its completion in a timely fashion. Imagine a mind that is so attuned to the world around you that you experience divine coincidences guiding your destiny every day. Imagine having such faith in your ability to walk out into the unknown, that you create the next chapter of your life with even greater vitality than the one you're leaving behind.

This is the magic of living transfunctionally. Once you have cleared out defunctional definitions of safety and security, you can live in a world where terrorism, economic quakes, pandemics and environmental catastrophes all exist, but you are no longer afraid. And the irony is, that in not being afraid, you don't become complacent—you become proactive. Changing your vibration from fear to faith galvanizes you to participate in a massive, evolutionary, collective change. Imagine feeling inner safety, a liberated life, and being a part of a joy filled, global family.

Imagine…

An Invitation

Dear Reader:

For an extended bio and more information about Dr. Toni Galardi's presentations or products, please visit her website, **LifeQuake.com** and **drtonigalardi.com**.

In addition, if you would like immediate contact for media opportunities, consulting services, workshops, or in-service trainings, please call 310-890-6832 and someone will assist you promptly.

Made in the USA
Columbia, SC
25 January 2023

75842566R10124